Marcel Proust

A l'ombre des jeunes filles en fleurs

Leighton Hodson

Senior Lecturer in French
University of Glasgow

UNIVERSITY OF GLASGOW
FRENCH AND GERMAN PUBLICATIONS
1994

University of Glasgow French and German Publications

Series Editors: Mark G. Ward (German)
Geoff Woollen (French)

Consultant Editors : Colin Smethurst
Kenneth Varty

Modern Languages Building, University of Glasgow,
Glasgow G12 8QL, Scotland.

In memoriam
Walter and Mary Hodson

First published 1994.

© UNIVERSITY OF GLASGOW FRENCH AND GERMAN PUBLICATIONS.

Printed by Castle Cary Press, Yeovil, Somerset.

ISBN 0 85261 444 6

Contents

Foreword

Most of the textual references made throughout this study are to the Garnier-Flammarion editions. That of *A l'ombre des jeunes en fleurs* is by Danièle Gasiglia-Laster (1987), in two volumes corresponding to what will be called Parts One and Two. Page references to it will appear in **bold** in parentheses, prefaced by I or II, e.g. (II, **94**). The punctuation marks of this edition have been scrupulously adhered to.

Longer titles have been abbreviated as follows:

La Recherche	*A la recherche du temps perdu*
Swann	*Du côté de chez Swann*
Jeunes filles	*A l'ombre des jeunes filles en fleurs*

The other parts of *La Recherche*—*Le Côté de Guermantes, Sodome et Gomorrhe, La Prisonnière, La Fugitive,* and *Le Temps retrouvé*—are given in full, as are any subdivisions of the work, e.g. *Combray, Un amour de Swann*.

Where other references are made to *La Recherche,* e.g. (Pléiade II, 421), they designate the earlier, Clarac edition (1954) listed in the Select Bibliography. Other page numbers in parentheses refer to the Pléiade editions of Proust's other works, and extracts from the Kolb edition of his *Correspondance* are designated by *Corr.,* plus the volume and page number. Quotations from items in the Select Bibliography are preceded by authors' names, and unless it is stated to the contrary, all italicized emphases are theirs.

I would like to acknowledge the help that, in preparing this manuscript for publication, I received from Angus Kennedy and Geoff Woollen.

Introduction

Imagine *La Recherche* to combine at one and the same time the qualities of a complex symphony and an undulating landscape, a landscape which has not only changing levels, but also changing lights that show up anew what we thought we were familiar with. Just as the complex symphony—to use an analogy Proust would have appreciated—can amaze us by the way the composer shifts our vision of his spiritual landscape, making us wonder how he has led us to some point of vantage and how he will contrive to move us on from it, so *La Recherche,* because of the quantity and richness of its digressive style, leads us to well-known, and sometimes less well-known, areas of the narrator's multilayered commentary on his own and other characters' behaviour and discoveries. In this respect, *Jeunes filles* more than any other part of *La Recherche* takes us to an especially well-placed part of that landscape. From this high point we can look back on the frequently trodden paths of *Combray,* and forward to the ever bleaker and ambiguous territories of *Le Côté de Guermantes,* of *Sodome et Gomorrhe,* of *La Prisonnière* and *La Fugitive,* then finally to the recuperative foothills of *Le Temps retrouvé* that lead to the shining heights of the narrator's justification for his existence. This he discovers with an emotional, yet rational, conviction that memory may be combined with an aesthetic which will be retrospective, all-encompassing and fulfilling.

The reader of *La Recherche* is constantly held aloft, in surveying the landscape below, by the sense of elation and euphoria that comes from the feeling of involvement in a high aesthetic adventure. Hovering over the opening pages on sleep and recollection, and then over the evocation of Combray is the narrator's longing for some kind of transcendence through the imagination. He finally manages, at the end of the *Combray* section, to express this, and experiences a short-lived literary triumph in his callow and excitable account of the Martinville steeples, in which, after being driven along in Dr. Percepied's carriage, he is able to give a kind of permanence to his sensation of movement as he relates to their changing position. He is particularly pleased with his little creation because he has achieved, alongside the crystallising of a numinous sense of place, a literary equivalent of the search for a meaning to his experience. In the next part, *Un amour de Swann,* the reader is alerted to the creative importance of music. During the excursion into the analysis of

Swann's jealous love for Odette the reader is always made aware, over and above the psychological intrigue, of Swann's confused emotional and critical response as he listens to Vinteuil's sonata. With *Jeunes filles* a third form of imaginary response is given pride of place: the visual. The role of Elstir, the painter, and his aesthetic practices not only parallel the narrator's frequent analyses of sensation and reality but also stimulate the reader, as did the use of Vinteuil's music, into examining aesthetic problems at the deepest level. The reader feels that the journey all along has been accompanied by the assumption of a well-informed and sensitive openness to the transformation of the observed world through art. To appreciate *La Recherche* we must be prepared to put a high value on aesthetic adventure. The narrator's eventual resolution of the search for lost and wasted time (in the double sense of the *temps perdu* of the title) is the discovery of the reunification of the apparently lost in an emotionally satisfying reconstruction which equates everything—the significant, the trivial, the grotesque or the sublime—with the beautiful. In Proust's vision of the world, art transforms and transcends everything and anything. *Jeunes filles,* above all parts of *La Recherche,* is devoted to an analysis and a celebration of the cardinal power of metamorphosis.

From the start, the key in reading Proust is that we should go along with this elevated tone of sublime aesthetic adventure, without forgetting that to Proust, though art is sublime, the material world it is made of and refers to may not be. Alongside the ideal, Proust has the keenest appreciation of the banal. He can integrate elevated sentiments with the weirdest of human relationships; indeed, his observed reality, as opposed to his high aesthetic, is firmly that of the everyday, from the pleasing to the sordid. Following on from the charm of the *Combray* section, where darker elements are only briefly alluded to, and *Un amour de Swann,* where they emerge more openly, *Jeunes filles* proves to be a good example of a characteristic duality in all Proust's writing that becomes increasingly evident in the later parts of *La Recherche:* a devious and obsessive paralleling of the sublime and the sordid like clean and brackish streams running side by side. To appreciate this on an aesthetic scale, imagine that the insight which Dickens is able to convey through the grotesque has been combined with a metaphysical longing for transcendence over the trappings of the real world worthy of the abstraction of Beethoven. All this, together with an eye and an ear for the comic, is expressed in an unforgettably evocative style that sets out to defy the dull greyness of time through the transformative power of the imagination.

In this explicative and appreciative study I intend to consider

Jeunes filles in a way that will make a richly layered text more easily accessible, and particularly so for a reader who until now has perhaps only read *Swann* and possibly parts of *Le Temps retrouvé*. I see *Jeunes filles* as extending, within the design of *La Recherche*, the adolescent enquiry of the narrator both in terms of sexuality and of his education in increasing aesthetic awareness. For this purpose it is as well to bear in mind the ways in which the sections of *La Recherche* can be grouped.

Proust always defended his novel against any charge of formlessness, claiming to have envisaged the end alongside the beginning in a grand scheme that had a complex, but nonetheless exact shape. When he published *Jeunes filles* in 1919, he re-issued *Swann* along with it. I propose, therefore, to take *Noms de pays: le nom* (published as part of *Swann*) together with the two parts of *Jeunes filles,* viz.: *Autour de Mme Swann* and *Noms de pays: le pays*. The final pages of *Noms de pays: le nom* have been linked with the opening of *La Recherche* as forming a parallel meditation on time (Stern, p. 9). Excellent though this suggestion is, *Noms de pays: le nom* can equally be taken as a prelude to *Jeunes filles,* as I suggest. This does nothing to diminish Proust's intention, nor does it distort any reading of the work, but rather reinforces the flexibility of interpretation that this novel, perhaps above all novels, invites. *Noms de pays: le nom* was intended by Proust to be an introduction to subsequent developments, although, at the time of its publication in *Swann* in 1913, it appeared to lead nowhere. In fact, it prepares for the importance of both Gilberte and Albertine as unsatisfactory adolescent relationships. It also dovetails perfectly into the fundamental theme of adolescent discovery and launches, in quintessentially Proustian vein, the idea of a name creating its dream around a reality that is yet to be concretely experienced. I shall seek, therefore, to make evident the often subtle parallels between *Jeunes filles* and the other parts of *La Recherche* in thematic material, the presentation of characters, and aesthetic theory.

For reasons of space in this short study, the discussion of autobiographical connections has been left aside. For the broad picture of Proust's career, reference should be made to the Biographical Table (pp. 86-9), which itemises concisely all the relevant information which the reader might need in order to elucidate points of chronology arising in this guide. The vexed question of Albertine / Agostinelli, or other male counterparts, has been deliberately avoided. The narrator of Proust's novel is understood throughout to be a fictional creation, and heterosexual.

Chapter One

Connections

So wide-ranging is any single part of each of the seven sections of *La Recherche* that the reader may only too easily feel disorientated. From this it is not far to a suspicion that the animal we are grappling with is slipping from our grasp, and might, indeed, have no coherent shape at all. The first reactions to both *Swann* and *Jeunes filles* were certainly a mixture of fascination and annoyance, reinforced by the rejection by some reviewers of a meticulously presented but amorphous mass. With the publication of *Jeunes filles,* Proust could look back to the mixed reactions he had received on *Swann.* While favourable remarks had come from friends, professional critics—however impressed they might have been by well-chosen detail—were particularly severe on the organisation of the text and on style. Typical of the kind of criticism which was prepared to accept originality but be rigorous on faults of presentation was the sarcastic review by the influential Paul Souday in *Le Temps,* December 1913, which looked forward to greater concision next time, should there be a sequel. Even more sharply critical of Proust's lack of form was the review by Henri Ghéon in *La Nouvelle Revue française,* January 1914, which described the work as drifting aimlessly along. To Ghéon, Proust, in being unable to reject anything, had spurned orderly shaping and produced the very opposite of a work of art. Since these were charges Proust was very sensitive about, he felt obliged to put up a defence by writing to both Souday and Ghéon to justify the seeming formlessness of what he had considered to be a carefully-planned work (*Corr.,* XII, 380-81). In particular, in writing to Ghéon, he was able to quote a letter from Francis Jammes that expressed the highest praise for a work that appeared to be a very model of form: '... on *peut* penser autrement que vous sur ce livre', as he put it (*Corr.,* XIII, 26). Jammes had combined percipience with such very high praise that it is not surprising that Proust was unable to resist repeating his remarks:

> Cette prodigieuse fresque toute fourmillante, qui s'accuse de plus en plus, cet inattendu des caractères, si *logique* dans son apparent illogisme, cette *phrase* à la Tacite, savante, subtile, équilibrée, voilà ce

génie qui se dessine en teintes maîtresses. L'abîme des cœurs. Vous y
fraternisez avec les plus grands. [...] Que vous nous fassiez pénétrer
avec une incroyable vérité dans la mordante jalousie de Swann etc. etc.
etc., j'y reconnais la griffe d'un maître. Qui donc a poussé l'analyse
jusque là? En France personne. C'est pourquoi il est regrettable
infiniment qu'on ne puisse répandre partout ce livre comme un modèle
de *forme, la plus savante* que je sache, comme un modèle d'analyse
sans égal. (*ibid*)

When *Jeunes filles* appeared in 1919 (with *Swann* re-issued
alongside it) the same criticisms remained and rankled. The whole
question was exacerbated by the reservations made widely in the
press over the award of the prestigious Prix Goncourt. Proust's slim
majority in the Prix Goncourt committee had given birth to such a
bitter controversy that critics could see little merit in a work which
had won Proust a coveted prize at the age of forty-eight when
younger, more readable and up-to-date talents were being ignored.
Hostile criticism of *Jeunes filles* was hard-hitting. It was described
by Rachilde in *Le Mercure de France*, January 1920, as over-long:
'Un livre trop long est toujours une impolitesse'. For Jean Pellerin
in *La Lanterne*, December 1919, it was also too demanding of the
reader's patience, a 'tissu serré de subtilités'. Again, the charge of
lumping together instead of selecting the material brought up for
Abel Hermant (*Le Figaro*, August 1919), the question whether it was
a work of art at all. Even though generally favourable in his review,
he considered that Proust risked creating a confused jumble and
assaulting the reader with sheer excess:

Il risque le fatras. Aujourd'hui qu'on ne veut que des livres courts, il a
le cynisme, je dirai même, pour employer un mot qui lui est cher, le
sadisme, de nous donner des volumes de quatre-cent-quarante-trois
pages à quarante-quatre lignes. Il semble tomber dans le panneau que sa
mémoire trop abondante lui tend.

A pastiche of *Jeunes filles* by the humorist Louis Léon-Martin in
Le Crapouillot, October 1919, entitled *A l'ombre d'un jeune
homme en boutons*, mocked the concern with pimply adolescence as
well as the excessive descriptive analysis and the narrator's sheer
inability to take any clear-cut decision. The send-up of Proust's style
is as sharp as Proust's own talent for verbal mimicry in this field.
By trivialising the content, Léon-Martin, just like Proust in his own
pastiches—and for the same critical purpose—lays bare the victim's
technique for all to see. He attempts to come to terms with what was
at one time, and perhaps still is, perceived to be a stumbling-block in
reading Proust. He makes fun of the inevitable adjunct to the riches
of complex comparisons by exaggerating Proust's inescapable

syntactical reliance on a whole series of qualifying phrases and parentheses. He cruelly exposes the mechanics of analysis and of constantly-deferred opinion:

> A ce moment l'idée me traversa que, puisque je me plaisais à l'ombre des jeunes filles en fleurs, je pourrais bien trouver quelque agrément à l'ombre d'un jeune homme en boutons, mais cette pensée fut immédiatement contre-balancée par cette autre que, si je n'hésitais pas, je n'aurais plus de raison d'écrire et qu'au surplus l'indécision est mon privilège, comme de couper les cheveux en quatre d'ailleurs, étant donné que je ne saurais perdre mon temps, attendu que l'on n'est pas sans ignorer l'incomparable emploi qu'avec un chapelet de considérations contradictoires je sais faire du temps même perdu.

Thematically, *Jeunes filles* was even mocked by Jean Pierrefeu in *Le Journal des Débats,* December 1919, as being unconnected with reality and stylistically as being a rag-bag of elusive trivia. A swingeing attack by Pierre Lasserre in *La Revue universelle,* July 1920, denounced its mannerisms and protracted comparisons, finding it particularly hard to forgive the combination of the impressionistic and the intellectual:

> M. Proust est le plus fallacieux des hommes. Il fait espérer à notre esprit de faciles plaisirs. Et que lui ménage-t-il en réalité? Des exercices sévères. Qui croirait que le livre qui ressemble le plus à un livre qui s'appelle *A l'ombre des jeunes filles en fleurs* soit *L'Éthique* de Spinoza?

While there were complimentary remarks from some reviewers on Proust's originality in capturing the precarious fragmenting of the narrator's experience, on the whole it is the awkwardness and the difficulty of the work that emerge most often from contemporary comments. Jacques Boulenger in *Mais l'art est difficile* (1921), saw him as remarkable, yet standing apart from the great French tradition:

> ... l'œuvre de M. Marcel Proust n'est pas composée, si peu que ce soit. Rien n'est plus contraire aux habitudes traditionnelles de la littérature française. [...] En France surtout, qui dit art, dit choix. Il n'y a pas, en effet, de beau roman qui ne soit 'vrai'; mais, d'autre part, toute la vérité n'est pas nécessairement belle: le goût choisit donc dans la vérité. [...] Le roman de M. Marcel Proust, incomparable dans le détail, est beau. Mais vu d'ensemble, à cause de ses disproportions, c'est un monstre—un beau monstre.

His 'beau monstre' seems to sum up exactly the ambivalence of contemporary feeling.

Some of these early impressions may linger today, yet taking into account the whole sequence, from *Noms de pays: le nom* through *Autour de Mme Swann* to *Noms de pays: le pays* , the modern reader is rewarded to see how very well put together the whole series is. There is a convincing presentation of the narrator as adolescent participant and mature commentator provided we appreciate the deceptive strength of the connective tissue that covers the work's ligaments. Richly varied it may be, but it is not always obvious. The very last manifestation of this connective material to seek in Proust, although it is the one most readers of novels first cry out for, is narrative line. This is distinctly and deliberately of secondary concern to Proust, whose prime objective is viewing reality from within the consciousness of the narrator. What gives the narrator cogency is not so much the telling of a story (though there are elements of that) but rather his attempt to justify his experience of people and comprehend his relationship to the natural world he perceives about him. Above all there is an emphasis on an obsessive learning process and a search for a method of transforming the experience of external phenomena into an aesthetic, and hence permanent, structure. I hope to show that what gives *Jeunes filles* its special dynamic quality, and saves it from being amorphous, is not the multiplicity of loose ends that offended early reviewers, but its complex network of subtle and sometimes subliminal interlocking connections. Take for instance Swann, in the two volumes that the first readers encountered in 1913. With no knowledge of *Jeunes filles* as the sequel, the reader could only be perplexed by *Noms de pays: le nom,* which appeared to lead nowhere. The confidential report by Jacques Madeleine for the publisher Fasquelle (published in *Le Figaro littéraire,* December 1966) poured scorn on a work that it was hardly possible to recommend for serious consideration :

> En somme, qu'est-ce? Pour quelqu'un qui n'est pas renseigné extérieurement c'est la monographie d'un petit garçon maladif, de système nerveux détraqué, d'une sensibilité, d'une impressionnabilité et d'une subtilité méditative exacerbées.
> C'est curieux, souvent. Mais trop long, disproportionné. On peut mettre en fait qu'il ne se trouvera pas un lecteur assez robuste pour suivre un quart d'heure, d'autant que l'auteur n'y aide pas par le caractère de sa phrase qui fuit de partout.

Yet, looked at with hindsight, we see that there is not only the pendant of *Noms de pays: le pays,* but also a clear balance within *Swann.* The opening pages on sleep form a prelude, followed by two major developments on Combray and Swann himself which are rounded off by a coda on the investigation of dream and reality suggested by names. Elements of the coda are subliminally planted in the mystery that surrounds Gilberte's name and in the way that the opening meditation answers the final pages on time (cf. Stern, p. 8). The strongest connective process of all—and Proust's greatest contribution to modernism—is the welding into the narration of a continuous commentary upon it. The commentator is a man in his forties who begins the process of evoking the past in the opening pages of the novel, embarking on the analysis and retrospective understanding of events in which he is represented as a younger self. There is a constant coming and going between these two selves, with the greatest weight being placed upon elucidation. Proust's originality is in this constant urge towards explication, and with it the invitation to the reader to function in tandem with it. We sense, particularly in *Jeunes filles,* that we are not reading about nostalgic re-creation so much as paralleling a self-discovery that any reader can share. We are observing from a mature point of view the very evolution of the adolescent and are present at those very moments of enquiry and discovery that, leaving aside the narrator's particular experience to which he has given a local habitation and a name, have a universal feel to them. We take part in his rites of passage.

What are the general characteristics we have to confront? Before coming to *Noms de pays: le nom* we have been prepared by the initial pages of *La Recherche.* These cover, in sequence: sleep, the emergence into wakeful consciousness, the drift towards reminiscence and a reconstruction of the past, first through voluntary memory and then, in the *madeleine* incident, through the more vivid involuntary memory. The *Combray* section which follows not only records childhood scenes and provides sketches of the adults the child encounters, but establishes within his inner life the importance of a response to the natural world and to sexuality. Proust is no sentimentalist interested in a coy return to the charm of childhood scenes; he brings out rather a viscerally alive, if shadowy, sensing of deeper and darker drives that the narrator has to come to terms with. Alongside his humorous «Zut, zut, zut, zut» in his impatience to 'tâcher de voir plus clair dans mon ravissement' (*Swann,* **266**) and his near-ecstatic lyrical response to the hawthorn blossom, there are the stirrings of sexuality. At first these are merely auto-erotic. The first notes of the eroticism theme involving others, which will develop and consume greater and greater space in subsequent volumes, centre at the outset on Gilberte; in addition there are the first *sotto voce* notes that prepare for the themes of sexual deviance that also assume greater and greater importance as *La Recherche* proceeds. Proust was aware from the start of the big problem he would have, with public and publisher alike, because he knew his work was indecent (*Corr.,* IX, 155-6). The quality of these first soundings is extremely important, for in them are hidden the overtones of a bruised and essentially sad experience. The references to Mlle Vinteuil and her girl-friend show in germ the combination of furtiveness, sadism and sadness that colour many of the personal relationships in *La Recherche*. While the narrator is to be shown free from sexual deviance, his experience in *Jeunes filles,* and especially in the later sections concerning Albertine, will be nevertheless bleak and tormenting. All Proust's characters, apart from Françoise, the mother, the grandmother and the family, will have unpleasant experiences in their personal relationships, whether hetero- or homosexual. Against these pessimistic notes the narrator places the counterpointing theme of hope: the hope of transcending the unpleasant and the evanescent sides of experience by the transfiguration of the contingent world in words. The imagination realised in works of art is the sole consolation, not only for contingency but for mortality itself.

Before *Jeunes filles* there is a further investigation of the combined theme of a love relationship and art. *Un amour de Swann*—the only part of *La Recherche* in the third person—charts the relationship of Swann and Odette, only to reveal its inherent destructiveness in the jealousy that becomes the driving force of Swann's experience of love. The consolations of art are present also, but they are perceived as decorative rather than vitally creative. Swann abandons his excursion into aesthetics by leaving undone his essay on Vermeer; and music, in this case Vinteuil's sonata, is at first exploited for its associative and sentimental powers. *Un amour de Swann* is both prelude and foil to the narrator's experience of love with Albertine. It takes the form of a brilliantly executed expression of the disappointments that lie in erotic experience, and develops on a heterosexual level the sadness and even cruelty that was hinted at in *Combray* in the case of Mlle Vinteuil. This attitude to the erotic will increase in force in the remainder of the novel with the result that erotic experience of any kind is fraught permanently with negative sensations: distance, not union, disappointment, not joy, degeneration, not mutually created passion.

Abandoning the third-person narrative of *Un amour de Swann,* Proust proceeds to the next part of *La Recherche, Noms de pays: le nom,* by resurrecting the first-person narrator. In doing so he brings out two attitudes that lay the foundation for *Jeunes filles.* The first is disappointment with a reality that fails to live up to a preconceived ideal. The second is the urge to find some overwhelming sensual experience so rich in itself that it transcends the inherent disappointment of the contingent world.

He starts anew the process of investigating the past with a technique similar to that used in the opening pages of the novel. Just

as the narrator had there referred to the main localities that the novel
is intended to cover by naming Balbec, Paris, Doncières and Venice
(*Swann,* **101**), so in resuming the narrator's story, Proust broaches
again the theme of remembering the bedrooms he associates with
different places, in this case the Grand-Hôtel de la Plage at Balbec. In
turn, a subsequent reverie on the association of place-names moves
naturally to the reverie on Gilberte's name, which he hears during
their games before properly knowing her. Taken together, these
remind us of the contrast between dream and reality already
prefigured in *Combray,* where the narrator weaves a dream around
the name Guermantes before seeing the actual Mme de Guermantes,
and in *Un amour de Swann,* where Swann associated Odette with
figures in painting and with music, thus distancing the real woman
from his fantasy. The theme of distance and dream also forms the
finale of *Noms de pays: le nom,* when the narrator evokes Swann,
transformed from elegant man of fashion into father of Gilberte, and
when he describes Mme Swann as an elevated and emblematic figure
riding in her carriage in the Bois de Boulogne. The description of
Mme Swann draws attention also to the different points of view in
the narrative which will recur in *Jeunes filles.* These have been aptly
described as 'a complex vision, compounded of Marcel's view as a
child, his later reflections on that naive view, and his view "now", as
a mature man. We end again (as in *Combray*) in that indefinite
"now", with the mature Marcel revisiting the Allée in nostalgic
mood, longing to recapture what is no longer to be found' (Minogue,
p. 16). The narrator concludes this section by evoking his sense of
disappointment with the present which can never live up to memory:

> ... le souvenir d'une certaine image n'est que le regret d'un certain
> instant; et les maisons, les routes, les avenues, sont fugitives, hélas,
> comme les années. (*Swann,* **573**)

The opening paragraph of *Noms de pays: le nom,* in its immediate
evocation of the sea, prepares us for Balbec but also, as we shall see,
in its imagery of fragmentation launches an important variation on
the theme of our perception of reality, and hence on the gap between
expectation and experience. What might appear as a piece of
decorative filling is in fact functional, in that it looks forward to the
importance of the image of the sea as a signal of changeability, the
very quality that is the pre-eminent mark of *Jeunes filles.* The
narrator describes the sea not by a conventional evocation of its
mass, but by reference to its individual fragments. He speaks of the
reflections of the sea in the glass panels of the bookcases lining the
walls of the narrator's bedroom, and emphasises the refraction of the
observed world not as a totality, but as discontinuous pieces, the

complete picture being in fact a composition we create for ourselves.
It is we who impose unity on what can only be perceived in
fragments:

> ... selon la place qu'elles occupaient [...] telle ou telle partie du tableau
> changeant de la mer se reflétait, déroulant une frise de claires marines,
> qu'interrompaient seuls les pleins de l'acajou. (*Swann*, 523)

The narrator has already illustrated this theme in *Combray* by
indicating his awareness of the discontinuous information we receive
not only of places, but of people such as Swann, who will shortly be
reassessed in his relation to Gilberte, and even more fundamentally
at the beginning of *Autour de Mme Swann*. The same image, where
the sunset on the sea is presented in an atomised form which the
mind has to fashion into a rational unit, recurs in *Noms de pays: le
pays,* coupled with the idea of an altar-painting divided into its
component parts that the imagination of the spectator has to
complete, thus resolving the discontinuity by a process that lies
outside the contingent world:

> Bientôt les jours diminuèrent et au moment où j'entrais dans la chambre,
> le ciel violet [...] s'inclinait vers la mer sur la charnière de l'horizon
> comme un tableau religieux au-dessus du maître-autel, tandis que les
> parties différentes du couchant exposées dans les glaces des
> bibliothèques basses d'acajou qui couraient le long des murs et que je
> rapportais par la pensée à la merveilleuse peinture dont elles étaient
> détachées, semblaient comme ces scènes différentes que quelque maître
> ancien exécuta jadis pour une confrérie sur une châsse et dont on exhibe
> à côté les uns des autres dans une salle de musée les volets séparés que
> l'imagination seule du visiteur remet à leur place sur les prédelles du
> retable. (II, 188)

Balancing this notion of the fractured perception of the contingent
world is the longing for a cohesive and overwhelming experience
which will transcend both fragmentation and dissatisfaction. The
narrator's dream is to be present at a storm at sea, especially at
Balbec, fancifully suggested to him by Legrandin as wrapped in mist
and mystery at the world's end. Swann, too, has evoked for him a
further expectation: a visit to Balbec church with its combination of
Gothic style and Oriental atmosphere. The narrator's greatest joy
would be to see the two together. Taken together, elemental nature
and cultural artefact are a token of a wholeness that can cancel
spiritual disappointment for, as he says of the storm:

> Je n'avais pas de plus grand désir que de voir une tempête sur la mer,
> moins comme un beau spectacle que comme un moment dévoilé de la
> vie réelle de la nature; ou plutôt il n'y avait pour moi de beaux spectacles
> que ceux que je savais qui n'étaient pas artificiellement combinés pour

> mon plaisir, mais étaient nécessaires, inchangeables—les beautés des
> paysages ou du grand art. [...] Alors, par les soirs orageux et doux de
> février, le vent—soufflant dans mon cœur, qu'il ne faisait pas trembler
> moins fort que la cheminée de ma chambre, le projet d'un voyage à
> Balbec—mêlait en moi le désir de l'architecture gothique avec celui
> d'une tempête sur la mer. (*Swann,* **524-6**)

Proust is expressing in condensed form in these opening pages of
Noms de pays: le nom what will become in *Jeunes filles* a firm
structure for the narrator's aesthetic development. On the one hand
there is the contrast between expectation and real experience (which
will be fully explored in relation to La Berma's performance,
Bergotte, the church at Balbec and even Albertine's kiss) and on the
other, the transformation of the elemental that the narrator senses
originating in the natural scenes around him, and that he will
discover has been realised by Elstir in his paintings.

There remains the creation of a starting point for the theme of
adolescent self-definition with regard to the opposite sex which will
gradually become the strongest theme of *Jeunes filles*. At first the
narrator's interest is shown to be centred on Gilberte. When he goes
to Balbec it moves to the group of girls, and eventually, though only
after a long process of trial and error, to Albertine. Proust prepares
us, before leaving *Noms de pays: le nom,* for this particular form of
self-discovery by describing the narrator's gradual and partial
knowledge of Gilberte. His interest first crystallises around her name
(*Swann,* **535**), in a long apostrophe to the mystery it evokes. A
similar effect is used later for Albertine (I, **179**; II, **192**). Central to
the narrator's experience is the gap between the image he has created
of Gilberte and the actual girl he plays with: they have become 'deux
êtres différents'(*Swann,* **543**). This prefigures the tormenting
changeability he will experience with regard to Albertine in *Jeunes
filles,* and even more so in *La Prisonnière* and *La Fugitive.* Proust
compresses the whole complex relationship of the narrator and
Gilberte into the simple image of the agate marble:

> J'achetai deux billes d'un sou. Je regardais avec admiration, lumineuses
> et captives dans une sébile isolée, les billes d'agate qui me semblaient
> précieuses parce qu'elles étaient souriantes et blondes comme des jeunes
> filles. [...] Elles avaient la transparence et le fondu de la vie. [...] je lui
> en désignai une qui avait la couleur de ses yeux. (*Swann,* **545**)

This image in itself prefigures, in its changing lights and lustrous
attraction, the theme of the insecurity of experience.

Chapter Two

Themes and Structure

The nature of the structural features that hold *Jeunes filles* together lies in themes and characterisation rather than in the sequence of events. Looked at in terms of what happens next, the work would not seem to present a problem, since a quick summary reveals that the events as such are unexciting to the point of dullness: the narrator meets Swann, Odette and Gilberte again and their acquaintances, Cottard, Norpois and Bergotte, sees La Berma on stage, goes to Balbec for a holiday with his grandmother, meets Mme de Villeparisis, Saint-Loup, Charlus, Bloch, Elstir, Albertine and her friends, and finally leaves as the hotel season comes to an end. What above all is important is the significance the narrator attaches to these events and his role in them.

Part One: *Autour de Mme Swann*

It is in this first part of *Jeunes filles* that the reader is made to see *La Recherche* not as something backward-looking and bathed in nostalgia, but concerned with physical and spiritual growth. All the earlier sections have been a preparation for the moment when the narrator's education gets truly under way. Up to this time he has been thought of as child (in *Combray*) or as in his early teens (in *Noms de pays: le nom*). As for *Un amour de Swann,* everything is supposed to have happened before he was born and can be set aside as part of his development. The Swann-Odette story is intended not as his experience but as a foil to what is later narrated about himself in relation notably to Albertine and his jealousy. Proust provides no specific dates or ages but it would appear that by the time of *Autour de Mme Swann* the narrator is rather more mature than at the time of playing with Gilberte on the Champs-Élysées and that by the time of his visit to Balbec, described as being two years after the end of his friendship with Gilberte, he is in his late teens. By this juncture, therefore, the reader of *La Recherche* is fully embarked on a sense of forward development, and even hope. Broadly speaking, the

quality of the comment by the narrator as older man is tenderly
watchful but more sharply critical than in *Combray*, though not yet
as bitter as it will become. It is not often appreciated that there is in
La Recherche a progressive darkening of the narrator's views of
himself and others, which is dramatically exploited in Proust's
carefully-arranged fiction. Against the moment when the narrator is
at his lowest ebb in *Le Temps retrouvé*, Proust juxtaposes, after the
wide-ranging arc that stretches from boy, through adolescent to
disillusioned maturity, the succession of the narrator's most powerful
epiphanies, which are brought about by involuntary memory and
lead to his sense of release and self-fulfilment in literary creation.

   As with *Noms de pays: le nom,* Proust derives yet again his
structural strength from thematic interplay rather than events. These
can be very briefly indicated: the narrator reassesses the characters
of the people he has met; M. de Norpois is invited to dinner; he goes
to see La Berma; he resumes his acquaintance with Gilberte and is
invited to the house; he meets Mme Swann, and through her
Bergotte, who has come to lunch; his friend Bloch takes him to a
'maison de rendez-vous'; his friendship with Gilberte gradually dies
in proportion as his resignation to this development grows; life
continues, with a feeling of openness to the future. Looked at as
transition of event to event, the effect can appear awkward, at best a
free fantasia of whatever comes to mind. Proust's own indication of
contents is not particularly helpful:

> Coup de barre et changement de direction dans les caractères—Le
> marquis de Norpois—Bergotte—Comment je cesse momentanément de
> voir Gilberte; première et légère esquisse du chagrin que cause une
> séparation et des progrès irréguliers de l'oubli. (Pléiade I, 431)

No mention here of Mme Swann, who gives her name to this section
and figures very importantly in it, not least in its finale. No mention
of La Berma. Looked at sequentially, the whole of *La Recherche,* not
just *Jeunes filles,* is open to the charge of arbitrariness. To some it
can still appear to be Proust's least appealing feature. However,
looked at thematically, even allowing for the cuts that Proust was
forced into accepting, there is a spiritual progress of a general order
which is consistent and accessible to the sympathetic reader.

   The overarching theme of *Autour de Mme Swann* is the
adjustment the narrator, in his naïve younger manifestation, learns to
make with regard to his knowledge of other people and what he can
learn from them. He has constantly to resolve a state of perplexity
and the reader is aware throughout of a series of knowingly
arranged confrontations: with Swann, Mme Swann, Cottard,
Norpois, La Berma, Bergotte, Bloch, and above all Gilberte. This

last, the most trying, is the culmination of the most troubling
adjustment for an adolescent, and will serve also as a preparation for
the more complex experience with Albertine, laden with greater
bewilderment, in Part Two.

At first the adjustment has to be made because of the *coup de
barre* phenomenon, in that new information demands reassessment of
previous conclusions and brings with it the lesson that people cannot
be presented simply as so many finalities, but as sources of potential
change. Movement, variability, freedom of development, flux, these
interconnecting strands constitute the ground theme of *Jeunes filles.*
Proust opens this part with the case of Swann, who, as husband of
Odette, has capitulated to bourgeois snobbery. He had already
become 'un personnage nouveau' for the narrator in *Noms de pays:
le nom* (*Swann,* **550**), as father of Gilberte rather than the
prestigious visitor at Combray associated with the shaming good-
night kiss episode. The social transformation is such that the Swann
who frequented the highest ranks of fashionable society is now glad
to say that: 'la femme d'un sous-chef de cabinet était venu rendre
visite à Mme Swann' (I, **86**). Likewise, in the case of Cottard, new
evidence means that a man once thought of (in *Un amour de Swann*)
as socially awkward and an utter fool (I, **87**) can also be a good
doctor, whose flair in diagnosis demands a complete realignment of
his reputation: '... nous comprîmes que cet imbécile était un grand
clinicien'.(I, **164**).

The series Norpois > La Berma > Bergotte shows the process of
adjustment as it occurs without the benefit of a time lapse. We are
present as the narrator discovers more subtle lessons in his
confrontations with people. His antennae of awareness have become
more sensitive, with the consequence that his observation is enriched
with both comic detachment and a shrewd reappraisal of his own
progress in judgement. Proust does not crudely state that the callow
youth matures, but reveals it as it actually happens.

The comic, linked to the theme of preparing the narrator's
spiritual development, is evident in Norpois. As a diplomat schooled
in the ways of manipulative language, he comes across through his
overblown pomposity as a misleading guide for the narrator. To the
narrator's parents he is the distinguished former ambassador and
friend of the family, impressive and urbane in his old-fashioned way.
To the narrator he becomes the embodiment of a certain kind of
misuse of language, of disdainful aloofness, and of an astuteness that
has turned into cattiness. As the narrator becomes sensitised to these
features of a professional wind-bag, Proust is also relaunching
another most important theme in *La Recherche:* the power of
language and what can be done with it. M. de Norpois exhibits not

the liberation that language can bring, but the danger of entrapment by it. He can be compared with the narrator's experience of Legrandin in *Combray* (*Swann*, **227**; **233**). The contrast that emerges here is that the language used by Norpois is as ossified as Bergotte's is creative:'il s'était imbu de cet esprit négatif, routinier, conservateur, dit «esprit de gouvernement»' (I, **90**). Norpois, in his advice on specific literary matters, betrays his total insensitivity to language. He prefers his own incommunicative orotundity to timely sympathy as he opines on the literary career of a young man of his acquaintance:

> Il a publié il y a deux ans—il est d'ailleurs beaucoup plus âgé que vous, naturellement—un ouvrage relatif au sentiment de l'Infini sur la rive occidentale du lac Victoria-Nyanza et cette année un opuscule moins important, mais conduit d'une plume alerte, parfois même acérée, sur le fusil à répétition dans l'armée bulgare, qui l'ont mis tout à fait hors de pair. [...] En somme, sans pouvoir dire encore qu'il soit au pinacle, il a conquis de haute lutte une fort jolie position et le succès qui ne va pas toujours qu'aux agités et aux brouillons, aux faiseurs d'embarras qui sont presque toujours des faiseurs, le succès a récompensé son effort. (I, **111**)

The contact with Norpois, however, is ambivalent. On the one hand, his advice on writing is non-existent. On being offered perusal of the narrator's literary efforts—the triumphant little essay on the Martinville steeples that had filled the narrator with at least temporary joy—he has no comment (I, **113**). On the other hand, all is not negative. It is his shrewd incidental remark on La Berma that helps the narrator make sense of his confused reactions to her performance in *Phèdre*. Norpois, then, is an example of an ambiguous guide to the narrator in his spiritual development and in his search for his literary vocation. We must think of him as being on the lowest rung of the guides the narrator encounters. From now on, they build in positive importance with the next two: La Berma, an executant artist in words, and Bergotte, the successful writer and his favourite author. Through all three of them emerges the theme of artistic revelation that prepares the narrator for his most important understanding of art so far, when he meets Elstir in Part Two.

   In the narrator's experience of La Berma and Bergotte, two themes are closely allied: both the potential excitement of what their art has to offer, and that fundamental feeling of an unhappy discrepancy between dream and reality. The narrator is not at first impressed on hearing La Berma in *Phèdre,* and discovers only on detachment from her performance and with hindsight how her art is not mere technical display, which he had wanted to find in a star, but due proportion and shaping (I, **106**; **142**). Similarly with Bergotte, there is the shock of meeting an admired author who, in person, seems the contrary of the subtle elegance of his style of writing. His appearance contradicts the image the narrator has built up in his reading. He experiences a comic deflation of all the elegant intelligence he had met in the books that had made him think of an old man, a 'doux Chantre aux cheveux blancs'. Instead he sees 'un homme jeune, rude, petit, râblé et myope, à nez rouge en forme de coquille de colimaçon et à barbiche noire' (I, 220). Proust brings together in the narrator's comments on this experience both the deception occasioned by the confrontation of the idealised and the real world, and the prime freedom of the imagination which can transform whatever it wishes and create new realities of its own. Here is a clinching of the whole problem of reality and imagination, a lesson to be more fully resolved in Part Two, when the narrator is confronted by the physical rendition of sea and sky in Elstir's transformations of Balbec. Proust brings in also another aspect of the theme dealing with the gap between ideal and real as he comments on the temptation and inadequacy of our desire to contradict the flow of things by labelling and naming. In due course he will make the startling discovery, on seeing Elstir's work, that the artist is not trapped by the contingent world around him, but transcends it by naming it anew through the interaction of his imagination and what he observes. The narrator's summing-up of his experience of meeting Bergotte becomes a springboard, not only for the more complex aesthetic discovery in Part Two, but for the whole of *La Recherche:*

> Sans doute, les noms sont des dessinateurs fantaisistes, nous donnant des gens et des pays des croquis si peu ressemblants que nous éprouvons souvent une sorte de stupeur quand nous avons devant nous au lieu du monde imaginé, le monde visible (qui d'ailleurs n'est pas le monde vrai, nos sens ne possédant pas beaucoup plus le don de la ressemblance que l'imagination, si bien que les dessins enfin approximatifs qu'on peut obtenir de la réalité sont au moins aussi différents du monde vu que celui-ci l'était du monde imaginé). (I, 221)

Further, in relation to Bergotte there is a cluster of material that subliminally gives structural strength to what can appear to be inconsequential developments. Just before the Bergotte episode, Proust has started up ideas on aesthetics that have their origin in the seemingly trivial. Later, however, these ideas come into their own as preparing the ground for profound questions that concern the art of the very work we are reading. Listening to Odette playing part of Vinteuil's sonata (I, 199-203), the narrator embarks on an investigation into the way we decipher our perceptions of imaginative material. This section on listening to music seems a digression, when in fact it is reinforcing the theme of the narrator's aesthetic education, for the problems here discussed at length are once again a foretaste of, and pendant to, the overwhelming visual discoveries to be made on seeing Elstir's paintings in Part Two. This essay on aesthetics broaches the question of novelty in art, in this case music, and the difficulty of understanding or appreciating it until a new public exists for it: 'Il faut que l'œuvre [...] crée elle-même sa postérité' (I, **202**). At this point the narrator comes near to understanding that a new language is needed for our traffic with new works of the imagination, but has not yet made the vital leap to saying what is uniquely the property of that language. Having come to terms with Bergotte the man and Bergotte the writer, the narrator then takes up again the question of novelty in art and its attendant problems, and this time starts up the idea of the necessity of obliqueness, of metaphor, as the only guarantor of originality, thus prefiguring the revelation awaiting him at the sight of Elstir's paintings. Bearing in mind that the reader has by this time already become familiar, to some extent at least, with this technique, it would seem that Proust's words are here almost an apologia for his style, not least for the greater dependence on metaphor that will be manifest in the subsequent parts of *La Recherche:*

> D'ailleurs toute nouveauté ayant pour condition l'élimination préalable du poncif auquel nous étions habitués et qui nous semblait la réalité même, toute conversation neuve, aussi bien que toute peinture, toute musique originales, paraîtra toujours alambiquée et fatigante. (I, **225**)

The cumulative effect is that, far from wandering from subject to subject, Proust has provided, like an underground stream resurfacing every so often, a cunning interlinking of the stages in the narrator's aesthetic education. This begins with the misuse of language by Norpois, and proceeds through La Berma's realisation of high dramatic art and the narrator's investigation into the complexities of new music to culminate in his understanding of the force of metaphor in Bergotte.

We have specimens of Norpois, of La Berma (through Racine), of Vinteuil (in the sense that there have been transcriptions of his sound world in *Un amour de Swann*), but no direct specimen of Bergotte. However, there is a stylistic analysis of Bergotte's writing in which the narrator himself has to resort to using metaphor to bring out Bergotte's uniqueness—an 'équivalent musical'—which is in itself a foretaste of the sea / land metaphor to be used by Elstir. Indeed, the narrator's conclusion on this point is a brief song of praise to the transformative power of the imagination that will be the lesson awaiting him in two years' time:

> De même ceux qui produisent des œuvres géniales ne sont pas ceux qui
> vivent dans le milieu le plus délicat, qui ont la conversation la plus
> brillante, la culture la plus étendue, mais ceux qui ont eu le pouvoir,
> cessant brusquement de vivre pour eux-mêmes, de rendre leur
> personnalité pareille à un miroir, de telle sorte que leur vie si médiocre
> d'ailleurs qu'elle pouvait être mondainement et même, dans un certain
> sens, intellectuellement parlant, s'y reflète, le génie consistant dans le
> pouvoir réfléchissant et non dans la qualité intrinsèque du spectacle
> reflété. (I, **228-9**).

Before leaving this section on Bergotte, the narrator broaches the
question of the morality of the artist—something to be discussed also
in relation to Elstir—and defends it in a formula that goes beyond
the lesson learnt by the adolescent from Bergotte. Proust actually
provides for himself a justification for creating the work we are
reading and hints, in the words 'vraie vie', at his personal dilemma
when he will be confronted by the mystery of the three trees at
Hudimesnil in Part Two:

> Et à ce problème l'artiste donne une solution non pas dans le plan de sa
> vie individuelle, mais de ce qui est pour lui sa vraie vie, une solution
> générale, littéraire. (I, **233**).

With Bloch and Gilberte, we move to themes that define
adolescent sexuality. It is through his friend Bloch that the narrator
is introduced to a 'maison de passe' and to the experience of sex as a
commodity (I, **253-6**). It is there that he meets «Rachel quand du
Seigneur», who is destined to play an important part in his friendship
with Saint-Loup and whose existence and life-style alert him to the
underside of sexuality, which in its various forms becomes a major
feature of his knowledge of people and a source of growing guilt. He
gives his Aunt Léonie's furniture to the 'entremetteuse' for purposes
that seem to desecrate the childhood associations of it in Combray,
and occasion perverse memories:

> Mais dès que je les retrouvai dans la maison où ces femmes se servaient
> d'eux, toutes les vertus qu'on respirait dans la chambre de ma tante à
> Combray, m'apparurent, suppliciées par le contact cruel auquel je les
> avais livrées sans défense! J'aurais fait violer une morte que je n'aurais
> pas souffert davantage. Je ne retournai plus chez l'entremetteuse, car ils
> me semblaient vivre et me supplier, comme ces objets en apparence
> inanimés d'un conte persan, dans lesquels sont enfermées des âmes qui
> subissent un martyre et implorent leur délivrance. D'ailleurs, comme
> notre mémoire ne nous présente pas d'habitude nos souvenirs dans leur
> suite chronologique, mais comme un reflet où l'ordre des parties est
> renversé, je me rappelai seulement beaucoup plus tard que c'était sur ce
> même canapé que bien des années auparavant j'avais connu pour la
> première fois les plaisirs de l'amour avec une de mes petites cousines
> [...]. (I, **255-6**)

This incident is embedded in, and contrasts with, the long finale of
Autour de Mme Swann describing the narrator's resuming of his
acquaintance with Gilberte, the resurgence of his love for her and its
gradual demise. This long analysis serves as a pre-echo of the finale
of Part Two, in which the narrator will linger over the ambivalence
of his feelings for Albertine. Surrounding this theme of the decay of
feelings, and resonating with it and with other themes, are three
subsidiary motifs that need to be clarified first: the elusiveness of
personality, the power of names, and the shift in the evaluation to be
made of a person's character.

First, in his attempt to define Gilberte, the narrator encounters
the difficulty that arises from any attempt by one individual to fix
permanently the meaning of the other, as if the other could be
arrested in his or her flux. Gilberte is perceived to be a mixture of
Swann and Odette, fluctuating between her parents: 'Il est vrai que
Gilberte était fille unique, mais il y avait, au moins, deux Gilberte'
(I, **241**). The features, physical and spiritual, that she shares with
them make her slippery and elusive, 'glissante comme une ondine' (I,
154). In a note in one of his working *Cahiers,* Proust is prepared to
associate her with the elusiveness of a water spirit (an ondine) and
compares her to Mélusine:

> Sur Gilberte au début. Elle avait quelque chose de glissant comme une
> ondine. Et son rire qui n'était pas toujours d'accord avec mes paroles
> semblait décrire une surface insaississable et délicieuse. Rappeler cela
> par une épithète quand je parle de la ressemblance de cette Mélusine avec
> sa mère. (*Cahier* 61)

In due course, the pendant love-affair with Albertine will repeat this
essential elusiveness of the other, and the evocation of that quality
will again be associated with sea imagery.

Secondly, the theme of names, so strongly built into the picture of
Gilberte, receives an ironical gloss in this section on the definition of
her personality. Swann has felt that a certain victory over death will
be achieved when his name will be carried on through Gilberte who
will become: 'Mme X., née Swann' (I, **243**). The reality will be
quite different, for Gilberte, unpredictable as ever, refuses this
association and will prefer to be known as Mlle de Forcheville.
Thirdly, the motif that picks up the *coup de barre* of the opening of
Autour de Mme Swann is the lurch in direction we feel when we are
obliged to reassess information and reset our judgement. Leading up
to the narrator's unpleasant discovery that his relationship with
Gilberte has to be re-examined, Proust as always prepares for the
major manifestation of a theme by lesser preliminary examples. The
narrator is primed for the grand finale by two telling incidents. He is

first made aware of the way life can turn things inside out when he
hears Bergotte's impolite remarks about Swann. The admirable
writer is a poor friend to gossip about Swann's private life:

> «Hé bien! c'est l'homme qui a épousé une fille, qui avale par jour
> cinquante couleuvres de femmes qui ne veulent pas recevoir la sienne,
> ou d'hommes qui ont couché avec elle. [...] » La malveillance avec
> laquelle Bergotte parlait ainsi à un étranger d'amis chez qui il était reçu
> depuis si longtemps était aussi nouvelle pour moi que le ton presque
> tendre que chez les Swann il prenait à tous moments avec eux. (I, **248**)

A comic version of the same jolt of reassessment occurs a little
later as a further variation—and one skilfully counterpointed—when
the narrator explains to his astounded family that the Swanns have
presented him to the bohemian Bergotte. However, since he is able to
point out that this individual, who seems to them to be beyond the
pale, thinks highly of his intelligence, the family begin to see virtue
where they once saw blame (I, **250-51**). Before proceeding more
deeply into the relationship of the narrator and Gilberte, Proust
completes this virtuoso playing with his subsidiary examples by
bringing out the change of stance the narrator himself is forced to
take up. He realises that the phenomenon of the *coup de barre* applies
to him as much as to others. Since all relationships must suffer the
law of discontinuity, what seemed settled between himself and
Gilberte can be overturned. He experiences in the intimacy of love
itself the signs of an alarming instability. Just as he thinks all
obstacles between Gilberte and himself have been removed, he is
shocked to discover that it is precisely from Gilberte that the new
change is originating and that his oscillation between joy and pain is
itself a further token of insecurity:

> En réalité, dans l'amour il y a une souffrance permanente, que la joie
> neutralise, rend virtuelle, ajourne, mais qui peut à tout moment devenir
> ce qu'elle serait depuis longtemps si l'on n'avait pas obtenu ce qu'on
> souhaitait, atroce (I, **260**).

The only conclusion is to accept a total reversal in their mutual
attitudes. In his dejection, and with a Racinian transformation of love
into hate, he refers to Gilberte's face, using an image that itself
mimics the precariousness and changeability of feelings:

> Quand elle était ainsi, quand un sourire ne remplissait pas ses yeux et ne
> découvrait pas son visage, on ne peut dire de quelle désolante
> monotonie étaient empreints ses yeux tristes et ses traits maussades. Sa
> figure, devenue presque laide, ressemblait alors à ces plages ennuyeuses
> où la mer retirée très loin vous fatigue d'un reflet toujours pareil que
> cerne un horizon immuable et borné (I, **262**).

The sea image announces a more complex association of the sea and a female figure: Albertine.

The ground is now clear for the finale of Part One of *Jeunes filles* (I, **291-329**). The lesser preliminary examples have chimed in well with the review of the narrator's feelings for Gilberte just as time is beginning to erode them. Everything strengthens the impression that we are about to watch the end of a relationship as it actually evolves from moment to moment. Proust's interest is less in the material (which is banal enough) than in the uniqueness of the process. The reader has a sense, in this part of *Jeunes filles,* of an extra value being put upon the data. More important than the data is the awareness the reader acquires of a general meaning that is made to emerge from the examination of the detail. Proust's originality comes fully to the fore in a way that has progressed well beyond *Swann.* This is the first time in *La Recherche,* excluding possibly parts of *Un amour de Swann,* where Proust's style and vision go into overdrive, carrying the reader along as if under a spell. There is not only suspension of disbelief, but also of rational reckoning until the process is over. The treatment of the Gilberte story here is a foretaste of a particular quality of enchantment that will be repeated in Part Two, again in the later parts of the Albertine story, and especially in *Le Temps retrouvé.* The final pages of Part One sustain at virtuoso level an unremitting analysis of the absence of the other. It is as if the reader is observing the narrator looking into an empty space, even though the gap for him is pregnant with the desire for Gilberte, for her return to him. He imagines what presents he will give her, what he will say, what letter she will write. Yet there is nothing before us but the ache of the narrator's loss, deeply and obsessively analysed and done in a way that redefines not only Gilberte's role (as absent), but more importantly his own as suffering the inevitable outcome of time's decay, that sense of the pain of discontinuity in a relationship that should have the safeguard and permanence of affection. The narrator totally convinces himself and, in his extrapolations, attempts to convince the reader too, of far-reaching generalities in what is, after all, only the calf-love of adolescents. So deeply hurt is he that not receiving a letter from Gilberte for the first of January convinces him not only that all is over, but that he, in his obsessional memory of Gilberte, is the direct agent of the death of the heart:

> La seule chose à laquelle je tinsse, mes relations avec Gilberte, c'est moi qui travaillais à les rendre impossibles en créant peu à peu, par la séparation prolongée d'avec mon amie, non pas son indifférence, mais,

ce qui reviendrait finalement au même, la mienne. C'etait à un long et cruel suicide du moi qui en moi-même aimait Gilberte que je m'acharnais avec continuité, avec la clairvoyance non seulement de ce que je faisais dans le présent, mais de ce qui en résulterait pour l'avenir [...]. (I, **293-4**)

He is led by the sheer intensity of this feeling to conclude, in a general observation on the human situation, that, even in the most intimate of relationships, there is an inevitable and unbridgeable gap. His formula: 'on est toujours détaché des êtres' (I, **294**) is the first sounding of that terrible sense of distance between the narrator and Albertine in *La Prisonnière* and in *La Fugitive* that will become his final view of all deep human involvement.

His experience of this bleak outlook is reinforced in his ironically loving attempt to bridge the gap by selling Aunt Léonie's fine vase so as to spend the money on Gilberte, only to discover, as he approaches the house in his cab, that she has just left and is walking along the Champs-Élysées with a young man: 'Où avaient-ils été? Que se disaient-ils dans le soir, de cet air confidentiel?' (I, **309**). The extrapolation he makes from this situation is true to his mood. Happiness with another person, he finds, is impossible, and even the slightest success, given time, will inevitably fail:

Le plus souvent nous continuons de nous évertuer et d'espérer quelque temps. Mais le bonheur ne peut jamais avoir lieu. Si les circonstances arrivent à être vaincues, la nature transporte la lutte du dehors au dedans et fait peu à peu changer assez notre cœur pour qu'il désire autre chose que ce qu'il va posséder. Et si la péripétie a été si rapide que notre cœur n'a pas eu le temps de changer, la nature ne désespère pas pour cela de nous vaincre, d'une manière plus tardive il est vrai, plus subtile, mais aussi efficace. C'est alors à la dernière seconde que la possession du bonheur nous est enlevée, ou plutôt c'est cette possession même que par une ruse diabolique la nature charge de détruire le bonheur. (I, **310**)

This is not the end of the matter. In the gap between two people there remains the tormenting subject of the secret life of the other. This has already been thoroughly examined in the case of Swann and Odette in *Un amour de Swann,* and will be examined later even more meticulously in the case of the narrator and Albertine. At this moment it already exercises the narrator to the point that he can see lurking in the freedom of the other the possibility of different attachments, and hence of jealousy (I, **311-18**). A particularly difficult moment—with a convergence at this point of the themes of time and memory—is the instant when memory supervenes to throw light on the past, happy event and its present realisation. He remembers the moment when he had roughly played behind the laurel bushes with Gilberte, struggling to retrieve his letter to Swann while Gilberte kept it behind her back, and in the rough and tumble had had a spontaneous orgasm, not quite sure whether she had knowingly encouraged him (I, **158**). He is now filled with jealousy to think of what she may be doing with the young man, and so much so that both past and present overflow with gall:

> On devient moral dès qu'on est malheureux. L'antipathie actuelle de Gilberte pour moi me sembla comme un châtiment infligé par la vie à cause de la conduite que j'avais eue ce jour-là. Les châtiments, on croit les éviter, parce qu'on fait attention aux voitures en traversant, qu'on évite les dangers. Mais il en est d'internes. L'accident vient du côté auquel on ne songeait pas, du dedans, du cœur. Les mots de Gilberte: «Si vous voulez, continuons à lutter» me firent horreur. Je l'imaginai telle, chez elle peut-être, dans la lingerie, avec le jeune homme que j'avais vu l'accompagnant dans l'avenue des Champs-Élysées. (I, **316**)

What is particularly bitter here is that with hindsight the narrator will come to realise that Gilberte was not in fact walking with a young man at that time, but with her friend Léa, a lesbian, dressed as a man.

It is in this finale to Part One that we encounter the germ of Proust's pessimism regarding human behaviour which is to grow to the proportions of a belief that every love affair is doomed. The narrator's affair with Albertine will lead him to conclude that his love for her was fatally presaged: 'Ainsi mon amour pour Albertine, tant qu'il en différât, était déjà inscrit dans mon amour pour Gilberte [...]'. (*Le Temps retrouvé*, **299-300**). He can even state with categorical solipsism:

> Les liens entre un être et nous n'existent que dans notre pensée. La mémoire en s'affaiblissssant les relâche, et, malgré l'illusion dont nous voudrions être dupes et dont, par amour [...] nous dupons les autres, nous existons seuls. L'homme est l'être qui ne peut sortir de soi, qui ne connaît les autres qu'en soi, et, en disant le contraire, ment. (*La Fugitive*, **85-6**)

When we see the extent to which the break with Gilberte can permeate the narrator's thought, we may counter the impetus of Proust's writing here and extricate ourselves from his spell by questioning the general lesson he seeks to extrapolate from the narrator's experience. The narrator's learning this lesson for himself is more acceptable than its projection as a general truth. What seems to drive him to inescapably logical conclusions, and what is evident in the decline of his relationship with Gilberte, is the intolerable state caused by the mystery of the other, by the unknowable, and, above all, by the uncontrolled; she is his first experience of the unpleasant side of what he desires from mutual love.

The final pages of Part One, in accordance with the title *Autour de Mme Swann,* return to near-ecstatic memories of Odette and her elegant life-style, especially the spectacle of her riding or walking in the Bois. This long, lyrical section (I, **321-9**) puts an end to the tone of psychological analysis, replaces Gilberte with a contrasting figure of what is once again idealised femininity, and rounds off Part One with a sense of gradual indifference. The torturing thoughts on what Gilberte has come to represent are temporarily laid aside.

Proust reflects what to him are the truths he wishes to impart by mimicking the effect not of climax, but of continuity. This technique establishes a particular quality of narration in *La Recherche* that becomes from this point onwards more and more prominent: open-endedness. This investigative speculation regarding Gilberte will be repeated with Albertine at the end of Part Two (cf. Tadié, p. 407). It is Proust's originality to be among the first in modern fiction to show that human relationships do not begin simplistically at a single point but coalesce from many 'beginnings', evolve freely in a multiplicity of ways, and finally drift towards new states rather than progress logically to a neat stop.

Part Two: *Noms de pays: le pays*

As the title tells us, we have moved from the expectation of Balbec to the reality of it. In addition, the themes of *Autour de Mme Swann* now receive their logical extension. This second panel of *Jeunes filles* has a sense of encountering new faces about it that makes it the most vibrant part of both the narrator's adolescent rites of passage and his progress in artistic understanding.

Both *Noms de pays: le nom* and *Autour de Mme Swann,* have as their background middle-class *mores* in an urban setting. *Noms de pays: le pays* presents the middle classes at play in a fashionable resort. This has as *its* backdrop the sea, which is frequently evoked and admired for its changing appearance. The sense of flux that the narrator has so far experienced here receives, in the numerous references to the sea, a metaphorical expression that constantly informs the narrator's growing awareness of his perception and assessment of the world about him. The reader becomes conscious in Part Two of a new landscape, a large canvas with figures moving about in an ambiguous setting of sea and land. The narrative rhythm repeats the effects of Part One in that we meet, in carefully-arranged sequence, the smart summer visitors to Balbec before Albertine emerges from the group of girls. Likewise, the same impetus is created in the narrator's analysis of himself and Albertine as occurred with Gilberte. Part Two will, in fact, conclude with a similar sense of detachment and bewilderment that will be eventually accepted with resignation in the hope of happy memories. As with *Autour de Mme Swann,* events as such have less impact than the effects they create in the narrator's inner life, and it is the interleaving of themes surrounding both the events and the people involved that ensures the forward development of Part Two and its overall shape. Unlike *Autour de Mme Swann,* however, imagery is much more in evidence and used as a means to strengthen the text as much as to decorate it.

Most of Part Two describes, after the train journey and its promise of something new, the arrival at the Grand-Hôtel de Balbec and how the narrator and his grand-mother settle in. Nearly two thirds of Part Two is covered by this, up to and including the meeting with Elstir and Albertine. The last third is totally devoted to the long process of defining the narrator's role in relation to the band of girls and the slow crystallisation of his feelings for Albertine.

This dry outline, however, gives little idea of the unique quality of this part of *La Recherche,* with its rich, sensuous atmosphere sustained over three hundred and fifty or so pages. *Noms de pays: le nom* and *Autour de Mme Swann* have opened up for the reader the narrator's inner landscape, especially emphasising the touching vulnerability of youth and the narrator's particular sensibility as it hardens with experience. By this stage, this young man begins to appear as a spiritual Candide, onto the tender blankness of whose mind and soul the contingent world projects ecstatic longings for some transcendence of the delicious and tormenting feelings that are so readily aroused in him, and so hard to pin down. Embedded in the early pages of Part Two, and growing out of the sense of release from the hitherto confining urban ambiance, are indications that show the narrator opening up to his sensual dreams in a landscape of natural sights and sounds. The process prepares, by means of generalised sexual fantasies, for the attempted physical realisation of his infatuation for the band of girls, and ultimately Albertine. The finale of Part Two, for all its tentativeness, acquires a similar obsessive force as did the final pages on Gilberte in Part One. Proust sets up this effect by intense descriptions of the narrator's sensual longings as he becomes acquainted with this new world of experiences once he is away from Paris. More than the fact of his being in Balbec, it is the subliminal dreaming and overt fantasising suggested by the stimulation of nature that establishes the principal overarching theme of Part Two: openness to inward discovery.

This openness is first expressed in his lingering attachment to Gilberte, which he now discovers has become an intermittent state, at times falling away through routine (*habitude*), at times freshly present through some spontaneous memory or association. What causes the break to be more definite is the acceptance of new ventures, ousting old links and liberating his mind. The journey to Balbec will effect precisely this. The first step towards new beginnings is the departure by train with his grandmother, but without his mother:

> Pour la première fois je sentais qu'il était possible que ma mère vécût sans moi, autrement que pour moi, d'une autre vie. (II, **14**).

Alongside the promise of new beginnings, Proust launches the theme of differentiation, and hence the most crucial stage in growing up. The narrator has now become aware of his mother as separate from himself though his grandmother remains as a surrogate mother to help him on his journey, indeed he describes kissing her as having the quality of 'un enfant qui tète' (II, **36**). Nevertheless, the social weaning that has taken place opens the way towards independent development and the eventual installation of a new female figure in his life, Albertine. In addition, he acquires an enthusiasm for the reception and presentation of the sense data that make up our experience. His grandmother, a great reader of the letters of Mme de Sévigné for their mother / daughter attachment, allows him to read her copy. These letters strike him by their aptness, but above all by the way they open his eyes to the recording of perceptions as they occur before reason tidies them up in logical explanations. This is a lesson he will learn soon from Elstir's handling of natural phenomena and esteem as a particular virtue of the artist. An element is added to the narrator's aesthetic development that is encapsulated in Wordsworth's formulation in 'The Tables Turned':

> Sweet is the lore that Nature brings;
> Our meddling intellect
> Mis-shapes the beauteous forms of things;
> We murder to dissect.

By this stage Proust has thrown together in the first few pages a nexus of themes: memory, oblivion, the adjustment of mental states, the breaking of new ground psychologically and spiritually. Not least there is a foretaste of the prime lesson the narrator will presently learn, when he encounters the imaginative recording of reality by Elstir as it is chaotically and freshly observed.

This rich conglomeration of themes leads to the most important

expression of openness—and one that will span Part Two—the
narrator's deepening sensuality. Proust sets this up as a series of
fantasies combining natural scenes and girls the narrator happens to
catch sight of and vaguely hankers after. The first of these links the
narrator's vision of sunrise from the windows of his meandering
train with his chance sighting of the *vendeuse de café au lait* at a
country station (II, 22-5). Both elements, the natural scene and his
desire for the girl, share that same elemental ecstasy—first heralded
in his longing to enjoy a mystical participation with the sight of a
storm at sea in *Noms de pays: le nom* (*Swann*, 524)—that has the
power to lift the narrrator out of his sense of contingency and
inadequacy. Proust harmonises, in a complex and richly evocative
way, details describing on the one hand the cloud colours that the
narrator can see from his train window and on the other his sexual
urgency. The sensuous colours, seemingly fixed, evolve, shift and
dissolve with a life of their own, constantly sounding the
fundamental note of change which is itself imitated in the movement
of the train changing direction and recasting the whole scene. The
narrator senses within him the imperative to make a whole out of
these unsatisfactory, fragmented perceptions. The narrator's initial
perception of the pink edge to the cloud has intensified to red and
moved to the window opposite:

> ... si bien que je passais mon temps à courir d'une fenêtre à l'autre pour
> rapprocher, pour rentoiler les fragments intermittents et opposites de
> mon beau matin écarlate et versatile et en avoir une vue totale et un
> tableau continu. (II, 22)

To this, rather as he had dreamed of the peasant girl in Méséglise
and the woods of Roussainville in *Combray*, the girl with her milk-
can is assimilated:

> Empourpré des reflets du matin, son visage était plus rose que le ciel. Je
> ressentis devant elle ce désir de vivre qui renaît en nous chaque fois que
> nous prenons de nouveau conscience de la beauté et du bonheur. (*ibid*)

The second episode involves his infatuation, at a distance, with the
daughter of a resident at the hotel, Mlle de Stermaria (II, 59-61).
Just as the sensuousness of the milk-girl had been associated with
Méséglise and the pink colour of the sky, so Mlle de Stermaria is
associated with the pink blush of the water-lilies of the river Vivonne
of his childhood (II, 60). Even more than with the milk-girl, the
narrator has a longing to penetrate the secret life of Mlle de
Stermaria and possess it in a magical landscape which is itself
impregnated with the girl's personality. As the narrator is carried

away by this fantasy, Proust is preparing us for the more successful pursuit of Albertine, also a figure in a landscape which has been impregnated in turn by her natural variability and mystery:

> Ensemble nous aurions parcouru cette île empreinte pour moi de tant de charme parce qu'elle avait enfermé la vie habituelle de Mlle de Stermaria et qu'elle reposait dans la mémoire de ses yeux. Car il me semblait que je ne l'aurais vraiment possédée que là, quand j'aurais traversé ces lieux qui l'enveloppaient de tant de souvenirs—voile que mon désir voulait arracher et de ceux que la nature interpose entre la femme et quelques êtres [...] afin que trompés par l'illusion de la posséder ainsi plus entière ils soient forcés de s'emparer d'abord des paysages au milieu desquels elle vit et qui, plus utiles pour leur imagination que le plaisir sensuel, n'eussent pas suffi pourtant, sans lui, à les attirer. (II, **60-61**).

The suggestion of an unattainable secrecy is finally evoked in the third of these sensual images: the narrator's catching sight of girls as he passes by in a carriage (II, **85-9**) and above all of *la belle pêcheuse* : 'Mais ce n'est pas seulement son corps que j'aurais voulu atteindre, c'était aussi la personne qui vivait en lui [...]' (II, **90**). The narrator attempts a kind of total possession of *la belle pêcheuse,* though it is also one he wishes mutually shared. He mentions the Marquise de Villeparisis and her carriage that is awaiting him, and in doing so senses that the girl is impressed by this connection and has returned his attention. It is enough to make him feel he has achieved a vicarious, indeed disembodied, possession of her that both grants him control and releases him from her spell:

> Je sentis que la pêcheuse se souviendrait de moi et se dissiper, avec mon effroi de ne pouvoir la retrouver, une partie de mon désir de la retrouver. Il me semblait que je venais de toucher sa personne avec des lèvres invisibles et que je lui avais plu. Et cette prise de force de son esprit, cette possession immatérielle, lui avait ôté de son mystère autant que fait la possession physique. (II, **91**)

This 'sexual' confrontation completes the preparation for the real experiences with Albertine, which likewise will have a quality of the 'possession immatérielle' about them; specifically, the failed kiss will leave open precisely the problem of possession and control. All these premonitory sexual reveries will come into their own in the finale of Part Two, to which they will add the deeper resonance of their involvement with a real girl as opposed to distant fantasies.

A second overarching theme, reinforcing its presence from as far back as *Noms de pays: le nom,* and dependent for its effect upon reiteration, is the fragmentation of perception and the bewilderment that this presents. Proust re-establishes this before embarking on a series of portraits of the people the narrator meets at Balbec, reminding us of its importance but also looking forward to its application to the narrator's very perception of the new characters who are introduced.

Each manifestation of the fragmentation theme in Part Two has, integrated with it, according to a technique we have seen before, a subordinate variation. The first of these concerns the narrator's realisation of what Balbec church is really like as opposed to the picture of it he had created in his imagination (II, 25-8). This restates the often-encountered sense of deception felt when dream confronts reality. Balbec church is not, the narrator discovers, magically set by the sea at Balbec-plage but alongside a boring tram junction. The narrator's evocation of his deception rhythmically mimics the disintegration of his imagined and ideal setting:

> Mais cette mer, qu'à cause de cela j'avais imaginée venant mourir au pied du vitrail, était à plus de cinq lieues de distance, à Balbec-plage, et, à côté de sa coupole, ce clocher que, parce que j'avais lu qu'il était lui-même une âpre falaise normande où s'amassaient les grains, où tournoyaient les oiseaux, je m'étais toujours représenté comme recevant à sa base la dernière écume des vagues soulevées, il se dressait sur une place où était l'embranchement de deux lignes de tramways, en face d'un Café qui portait, écrit en lettres d'or, le mot «Billard»; il se détachait sur un fond de maisons aux toits desquelles ne se mêlait aucun mât. (II, 26)

More expressively, the narrator's account of the famous statue of the Virgin, idealised as a unique and complete work of art, reflects not only deception, but its reduction to a piecemeal assembly of banalities:

> ... mon esprit qui avait dressé la Vierge du Porche hors des reproductions que j'en avais eues sous les yeux [...] s'étonnait de voir la statue qu'il avait mille fois sculptée réduite maintenant à sa propre apparence de pierre [...] et c'était elle enfin l'œuvre d'art immortelle et si longtemps désirée, que je trouvais métamorphosée, ainsi que l'église elle-même, en une petite vieille de pierre dont je pouvais mesurer la hauteur et compter les rides. (II, 27-8).

The second manifestation of fragmentation entails the notion of parallax in relation to oneself and the people who impinge on one's consciousness. This is reminiscent of the *coup de barre* at the beginning of *Autour de Mme Swann,* but instead of a character being modified by new knowledge, it is the narrator who senses that reality—seemingly objective—has changed around him. This establishes the key notion of the observer's position in relation to those he observes, much as we insist on seeing the stars in a fixed plane such as the Plough or Orion's Belt, etc., when the components of each constellation are light years away from each other and, when viewed in a different plane, no longer suggestive of their traditional shape. The essential idea is one of restructuring:

> Il n'est peut-être rien qui donne plus l'impression de la réalité de ce qui nous est extérieur, que le changement de la position, par rapport à nous, d'une personne même insignifiante, avant que nous l'ayons connue, et après. (I, **33-4**)

This is a formula that Proust has, of course, put to use in earlier sections of *La Recherche,* where the difficulty of describing an individual completely has already raised unsettling questions about the security of our knowledge of others, and especially drawn attention to the literary problem of the recording of our judgement of them. The particular example is the case in *Combray* of Swann, who can be seen at the outset to be the paradigm for many future instances: 'nous ne sommes pas un tout matériellement constitué, identique pour tout le monde [...]' (*Swann,* 113). At this point in *Jeunes filles,* Proust is preparing us for the puzzling conclusions the narrator will presently reach concerning Mme de Villeparisis, Saint-Loup, Charlus, Elstir, Odette and Albertine.

Third in this series of fragmentations is a reminder of the idea launched at the beginning of *Noms de pays: le nom* in the description of light refracted in the panes of the bookcases (*Swann,* **523**). A neatly-expressed instance involves the narrator's description of the effect of light in his grandmother's room as 'un prisme où se décomposaient les couleurs de la lumière du dehors' (II, **77**) while he looks out on the ever-changing sea. When Proust makes a specific return to the image of light refracted in the glass of the bookcases and in the window in the narrator's hotel room (II, **41-4**), he leads on to a full-scale application of this prismatic, shattered vision which is the way we actually experience the real world. What could appear as a homogeneous element, the sea, is broken up into interacting pieces. Stillness becomes movement in a transformation of the separate reflections of the foaming, turbulent and sunlit sea into a wild mountain landscape of shifting peaks and vales. This apprehension of nature in its immediacy prepares us for the freshness of vision the narrator will discover in the intermingling of sea and land in Elstir's seascapes, but at the same time it gives full expression once again to the delight in those elemental forces that have the intrinsic power to grant exhilaration and joy.

A further reference to this same phenomenon, in which the effects of sunset are refracted in the panes of the bookcases and resemble panels of a complex altar painting (II, **188**), has even occasioned the view that we have here a metaphor that underpins the whole of *La Recherche:* 'Car les vitres de la bibliothèque basse de Balbec ne reflètent pas seulement les «parties différentes» du couchant: elles reproduisent encore et encadrent figurativement les diverses parties du roman entier' (Poulet 2, p. 129).

Ultimately what Proust is evoking through this theme of the fragmentation of perception is the lesson that perception is never simple and never complete, but rather the result of a continuous effort of construction, less a gift than the product of work, the work of imagination, i.e. the transformation of raw material. In addition to the example of the sea-as-mountain, Proust provides the description of the church at Carqueville which encapsulates the importance of this process of involvement, and hence of work. The description of the narrator's reconstruction of this building in his mind's eye by atomising its parts and guessing at the position of arch or window, even though they are obscured by ivy, sets a basic pattern for more personal observations that the narrator will make later, such as trying to decide exactly the contours of Albertine's physiognomy and especially where exactly to place her beauty spot. In his conclusion, for all that he accepts the need for deciphering—'il fallait pour reconnaître une église faire un effort qui me fît serrer de plus près l'idée d'église' (II, **89**)—the narrator re-establishes the unity of just proportion that can at times lie hidden beneath what immediately strikes the eye. Again, what might have appeared as a digressive description of an ivy-clad church of mere picturesque interest becomes a revelation of structural strength. It is precisely this 'work', of penetration beneath outer appearances, that will be essential to the narrator's gradual realisation of the worth of Elstir, and especially of Albertine, obscured as she is at first (like Carqueville church under its ivy) by the personalities of the band of girls that surround her. Our relationship to our perceptions is never passive. The narrator learns to strive with them, not only because they are bewildering—something that will certainly be true of Albertine—but also in order to yield to the harmonious beauty which the process of deciphering may create. In the same way, a breath of wind can penetrate the leaves that cover the static church façade and give the whole solid building the pulse of life:

> Mais alors un peu de vent soufflait, faisait frémir le porche mobile que parcouraient des remous propagés et tremblants comme une clarté; les feuilles déferlaient les unes contre les autres; et frissonnante, la façade végétale entraînait avec elle les piliers onduleux, caressés et fuyants. (II, **90**)

The nature of the narrator's enquiry so far has emphasised his development as being very much turned in on himself. Proust now starts up a series of examinations of relationships the narrator has with guests at the hotel, with the accent placed more obviously on his awareness of others. While this openness ultimately leads to a personal deepening of experience, the narrator has first to come to terms socially with worlds that lie outside his own introversion. So far the furthest point that the adolescent has reached is a tentative break from his mother and grandmother in the daydreaming that crystallised on the milk-girl, on Mlle Stermaria and on *la belle· pêcheuse,* the disembodied nature of which was still distant from real impingement on the self. His closest contact in this new area of adolescence, other than Gilberte, is *la belle pêcheuse,* and that is at a safe remove. The proper conclusion to this stage of development can, of course, only be his eventual association with Albertine, but Proust holds up that phase, which will be reserved for the finale of Part Two, by first digging deeper into the narrator's social education.

This is done in a series of adjustments towards a selected group of people who are graded to represent the problems the adolescent 'innocent' has to encounter. These problems can only be resolved by extracting sense from the bewilderment he experiences. The sequence is so arranged that the narrator is observed in the processss of becoming wiser in the ways of the world, and hence maturing, before being put to the final test of his intimate investigation of his feelings for the girls, and especially Albertine. The people the narrator meets at Balbec are each associated with challenges in a particular order: Mme de Villeparisis with snobbery and also with the relationship of life to art; Saint-Loup and Bloch with friendship; Charlus with the mystery of the secret layers of personality; Elstir with imagination and the roles of public artist and private individual; and finally, the band of girls with the definition of the self in relation to the group.

The marquise de Villeparisis has a double lesson to teach the narrator. First, in her condescension (aided and abetted by the princesse de Luxembourg) she represents the world of snobbery and rigid class distinction to be opened up more fully in *Le Côté deGuermantes* and eventually shown, as *La Recherche* comes to a close, to degenerate under the weight of its own fatuous triviality. Suggestions that the narrator has to adjust his middle-class status to a superior nobility begin to emerge in *Jeunes filles,* when he meets Robert de Saint-Loup and the baron de Charlus and learns to match his privileged existence to the pride of an even more privileged one. Though he had previously dreamed as a boy in Combray about the name of the duchesse de Guermantes, this is the first real acquaintance with members of that world. It is the resumption of that long theme of snobbery that leads from *Swann* to the breakdown of

rigid class barriers in *Le Temps retrouvé,* with the ridiculous
upward mobility of Mme Verdurin who becomes, by widowhood,
marriage, second widowhood and remarriage, first duchesse de
Duras and finally princesse de Guermantes. Proust will ultimately
use it as an indicator of the degeneration of the hierarchical barriers
of society even as the narrator receives the final illumination of his
triumph over time and the distractions of Vanity Fair.

Secondly, and of more immediate importance for *Jeunes filles* and
the narrator's aesthetic development, Mme de Villeparisis represents
the world of taste and the arts, especially literature. She is privileged
to have had associations with writers of stature but, just as happened
with M. de Norpois, there is a terrible shortcoming. Her example,
like his, is not that of an illuminating guide. Her relationship to
literature is not to the work but to the man; she makes the same
mistake as Sainte-Beuve and confuses the social man with the creative
one. She gets no nearer to literature than biography will allow and
limits critical assessment to mere gossip (II, **84**). Her remarks on
Chateaubriand, Vigny and Musset are amusingly snobbish but
irrelevant (II, **96-8**). This is a lesson the narrator must unlearn.
Proust, for his part, had already done so, of course, in his
preparatory work, *Contre Sainte-Beuve* (published posthumously),
from which the immediate source of *La Recherche* can be said to
spring.

The treatment of Saint-Loup and Bloch shows the narrator's
contrasting attitudes to friendship. Saint-Loup, the coldly distant,
handsome and aristocratic nephew of Mme de Villeparisis becomes
eventually a close friend, and the narrator will feel that his
admiration for this seemingly unattainable person is returned.
However, the closeness of the friendship is not mutual, for the
narrator protects himself from that commitment by a reserve that
resents any surrender of any part of himself. He suffers a kind of
remorse 'de ne pas être resté seul et prêt enfin à travailler' (II, **113**).
Proust is hinting at the necessity for the artist to give away nothing
of himself and to direct his total personality towards creativity. This
is the first clear statement of a core theme, the difficulty of
surrendering a part of the self to the other, that will be the outcome
of the narrator's affair with Albertine. It is experienced here as an
element in the tentativeness and insecurity of adolescent emotions,
but at the same time it prepares for that eventual inability to make
any mature commitment to another person which will be a particular
feature of the narrator's failure, on a personal level, to know
positive and deeply-shared interdependence. His touchingly expressed
regret that he enjoys seeing Saint-Loup at a remove as 'un objet que
ma rêverie cherchait à approfondir' or as 'une œuvre d'art' (II, **114**)

both defines his adolescent failure at this point and foreshadows that scene in *La Prisonnière* where he observes Albertine asleep, at one and the same time near him and far from him, as a mere object.

Though he lacks the narrator's sensitivity and potential creative talent, Bloch, his Jewish friend is presented as a foil to the narrator's introversion and its dangerous tendency to encourage a stultifying inertia. He is so ebullient, down-to-earth and ambitious that he refreshingly replaces the agonies of adolescent emotionality, and especially the kind of indeciseveness the narrator experiences over Saint-Loup, by a vigorous sense of getting on with life and enjoying it (II, **115-25**). These two portraits map out two poles between which the narrator learns to define himself in relation to coevals of his own sex, and dispose in a clear-cut way of that particular aspect of his adolescence, before the more complex definitions of himself that he is obliged to make in relation to the girls. They allow Proust to adjust his narrative to provide a sense of progression towards a new threshold of experience.

Before moving on to that final stage, Proust presents the narrator with Charlus and Elstir, two characters who help to complete that part of youthful adjustment that has to do, not so much with people of the narrator's own age, but with mature personalities who are no longer in a state of becoming but who have arrived at a 'fixed' state. Charlus and Elstir have in common a challenge to throw down to the narrator: they both have a secret side to their lives which taxes the narrator's curiosity. Proust has already prepared the reader for this in the example of Swann but here he shows how the adolescent is excitedly caught up in sniffing out what intrigues him in the sheer strangeness of the behaviour, the coded signals and the values of an older generation. Charlus and Elstir provide the final stage in self-definition before the meeting with Albertine and the consequences that follow from that. In the subsequent volumes of *La Recherche* the outlines represented by these first sketches of these two characters will be elaborated and deepened, but all the new discoveries that the narrator will make are essentially stated here.

Proust has already shown in *Swann*, in his descriptions of Legrandin, Mme Verdurin and others, how behaviour, while being openly flaunted by the character concerned, is loaded, unbeknown to him or her, with countless signals. Some of these are obvious, some seemingly hidden yet betraying their presence, some subtly subliminal, some hopefully suppressed, yet to the keen observer not suppressed enough. It is for the interpretation of these—before Freud—that Proust has a particular predilection, and in addition a fine executant skill that he is able to exercise as needed, either to dramatic, even tragic, effect or with a light comic touch. Legrandin's

fleshy rippling rump in *Combray*—'cette ondulation de pure
matière, ce flot charnel'—is an amusing and memorable instance and
one that provides the ultimate statement about his attempt to hide his
servile snobbery as he goes through the motions of his exaggerated
bow (*Swann*, **232**). In the case of Charlus, Proust latches on, with
the skill and ruthless directness of a caricaturist of Dickensian force,
to yet another physical feature that will localise and epitomise a
moral quality. Legrandin's ridiculous bottom and Mme Verdurin's
absurdly dislocated jaw provide a comic distancing that fully suits
Proust's satiric purpose. With Charlus, that physical feature is the
eyes. His fixed stare, while being to some extent comically grotesque,
is more than anything an encapsulation of a tragic and furtive
isolation. Charlus exhibits a theme that increases in force as *La
Recherche* progresses: outward respectability as a cover for secret
sexual proclivities that in turn forms a part of the broader theme of
the deceptive face of reality. Charlus is seemingly an integrated
element of the social group represented here by members of his
family, Mme de Villeparisis and Saint-Loup, yet his behaviour
betrays to the narrator a suggestion that reality is not what it seems
on the surface. The truth is that, far from being integrated with the
group, Charlus is secretly separated from them by the gulf of his
covert sexuality. Proust is quite clearly sounding the theme of sexual
deviance as a mode of existence that must be cloaked in solitariness.
What had been obliquely touched on in *Swann*, in reference to Mlle
Vinteuil and her girl-friend, is here pointedly evoked as a secret life
peeping through a defensive barrier and characterised by a
precarious volatility that could at any moment erupt and disturb
tranquil appearances. Proust makes his point in a most telling image:
the suggestion of someone hiding behind the arrow-slit of a castle
wall, with true feelings being evident only in the glint of the eyes
themselves:

> ... les yeux étaient comme une lézarde, comme une meurtrière que seule
> il n'avait pu boucher et par laquelle, selon le point où on était placé par
> rapport à lui, on se sentait brusquement croisé du reflet de quelque engin
> intérieur qui semblait n'avoir rien de rassurant, même pour celui qui,
> sans en être absolument maître, le porterait en soi, à l'état d'équilibre
> instable et toujours sur le point d'éclater [...]. (II, **141**)

The first meeting with Elstir has at its core the aesthetic discovery
the narrator will make on seeing his paintings. The lesson is both
aesthetic and moral for the artist makes clear, to those who respond
to his paintings, that the world makes sense only in the celebration of
the contradictory relationships of its parts. The narrator has just
been shown as coming up against precisely this illogicality in his

encounter with the enigmatic stare of Charlus. He makes no further progresss for the time being in the area of understanding character, but the theme of his education shifts to the aesthetic problem of how mysteries, and especially contradictions, may be expressed and resolved through some artistic medium. Proust is here cumulatively bringing together elements in the narrator's progress in which Elstir represents the latest stage in a strand of development that has been going on from the Martinville steeples episode, through Bergotte, La Berma and Vinteuil (whose music is destined to play an even more important role in the narrator's understanding in later parts of *La Recherche*).

The aspect of the narrator's education which is given pride of place here is the realisation through visual art not only of a technique of representation, but also of a philosophical understanding of the relationship of the observer to the reality observed. It is this problem that has been shown to be the narrator's permanent interest, whether it has concerned his own sense of the visual, such as his attempts to understand exactly his pleasure in the sight of the hawthorn blossom, or his malaise in fitting together the disparate elements he has noticed in the behaviour of the people he has encountered. The case of Elstir actually brings together the two concerns since the narrator is confronted both with an element of aesthetic progress and the enigma of Elstir's character, which is itself based on contradictions. Both in his work and in his behaviour Elstir reiterates the theme that is ever present for the reader: never be satisfied with taking things at their face value. By placing the visit to Elstir after the encounter with Charlus, Proust is getting the maximum effect out of this theme, since he can suspend for a while the enigma of the truth about Charlus and proceed to another enigma, Elstir, and examine how the strangeness of reality can be resolved. Elstir's achievement is that he can see the port of Carquethuit as encapsulating the problem of opposites which, though apparent negations of each other in real life, can become in a work imagination elements that may be combined positively into a new statement. It is this new statement that penetrates the truth of the reality as originally perceived. In presenting the port of Carquethuit not as a photographic representation, but as an interchange of land and sea, Elstir thereby conveys not surface appearance but its essential truth as the intermingling of its several parts. Elstir's painting is not the prosaic, ordered apportioning of visual elements to make a particular geographical place; it is rather the most important statement in the novel so far, to wit: reality has its meaning only in the transformation of its parts. The banal port has been worked on by Elstir's imagination and his pictorial technique has metamorphosed it into the very emblem of how the contradictions of reality can be resolved through an artistic vision. This vision can equate the thing seen with the manner of recording it so as to transmit a fundamental philosophical point: only imagination combined with executant skill can bring form and content together to say that reality is not a thing given to us, but something created by our interaction with it. Elstir's paintings are the first fruits of that longed-for aesthetic control of reality that the narrator aspires to and finally creates for himself. Proust exploits the juxtaposition of Charlus and Elstir in this part of the novel to contrast the mystery of personality in Charlus with the mystery of the transformation of the confusing appearances of reality by Elstir's art. Through imagination, Elstir can make sense of contradictory elements and the feeling of disintegration by taming the discontinuities of reality in a renaming of parts by means of his own language:the medium of paint (II, 223). In his rereading / renaming of the world which he depicts he has both created a painting and realised himself. Furthermore, to top the theme of the revelation of a secret life, the narrator discovers that the successful artist, Elstir, is none other than the apprentice painter, M. Biche, of Mme Verdurin's salon and that the portrait of *Miss Sacripant* is that of Odette. As this secret falls into place we are reminded of other adjustments that have been heralded as far back as the *coup de barre* of *Autour de Mme Swann*. Discovering the true identity of Elstir is part of a recurring theme of transformations and incarnations. At this point it is reinforced by Elstir's own comment on the narrator's realisation of his past life as the immature M. Biche. It is not enough for Elstir simply to acknowledge the past. He can do much more and derive from it the important principle which in turn becomes part of the narrator's evolution: do not look back to the past without transforming it by inner reflection.

It is in the final third of *Noms de pays: le pays* that Proust brings all his thematic threads together, thereby structurally tying in all the suggestions of adolescent malaise. All the themes cluster around the way the narrator finally gets to know Albertine. Ingeniously, Proust uses Elstir both as the instrument by which the narrator actually meets Albertine and as the important spiritual guide in the narrator's development at this point. Since the fundamental lesson that Elstir has to teach him is the resolution of apparently disparate things, this is the very way he accommodates the presence of Albertine in his world. No sooner has he come face to face with her at Elstir's studio than his first cognisance of her is as the link, like a rainbow, between the contingent world of the girl in the polo cap with piercing eyes and chubby cheeks and the world of his deepest emotions. Proust uses in his description precisely the term that the narrator has

derived from seeing those of Elstir's marine paintings which had
blended land and water—'*terraqué*':

> Tout à coup y apparut, le suivant à pas rapides, la jeune cycliste de la
> petitie bande avec, sur ses cheveux noirs, son polo abaissé vers ses
> grosses joues, ses yeux gais et un peu insistants; et dans ce sentier
> fortuné miraculeusement rempli de douces promesses, je la vis sous les
> arbres, adresser à Elstir un salut souriant d'amie, arc-en-ciel qui unit
> pour moi notre monde terraqué à des régions que j'avais jugées jusque-
> là inaccessibles. (II, **233**)

It is in this encounter that the book gathers force to home in on a
conclusion. What could have appeared amorphous has behind it the
firm intention to seek a resolution, if only a temporary one, of what
the stay at Balbec has meant to the narrator:—sensuality, the physical
coming to terms with idealised dreams and the great potential of the
fertile interplay of meanings in the perceived world, whether of
people or things that has gradually emerged from meeting Saint-
Loup, Charlus, and above all Elstir.

In setting up his finale, Proust provides links and parallels with
the narrator's acquaintance with Gilberte so as to invite comparison
between the early adolescent experience and the later, more sexually
alert experience, with Albertine. The narrator is, in fact, laying the
foundations for the intermingling of Gilberte and Albertine. Gilberte
remembers Albertine at school with her reputation as being 'très
«fast»' (I, **179**). The overlap eventually reaches the point in *La
Fugitive* where Gilberte sends him the letter in which he misreads
her signature as being Albertine's. The confusion over Gilberte's
signature is already prepared in the way Françoise reads A for the
flourish of her elaborate 'G historié' (I, **167**). The two become, to
the the narrator and to the reader, almost a composite character who
has aptly been described as 'Gilbertine' (Willis, p. 342). Even the
kiss, of which much is made in the episode at the Grand-Hôtel, was at
first associated with Gilberte (Whiteley, p. 23). Proust has given a
certain structural strength and inevitablity to this association of the
two girls by preparing the reader as early as *Autour de Mme
Swann,* when the narrator refers to the dinner he had declined to
attend because of Gilberte where he might well have met Albertine.
He links the two girls by sounding the common ground-note of the
potential for unhappiness:

> Les différentes périodes de notre vie se chevauchent ainsi l'une l'autre.
> On refuse dédaigneusement, à cause de ce qu'on aime et qui vous sera
> un jour si égal, de voir ce qui vous est égal aujourd'hui, qu'on aimera
> demain, qu'on aurait peut-être pu, si on avait consenti à le voir, aimer
> plus tôt, et qui eût ainsi abrégé vos souffrances actuelles, pour les
> remplacer, il est vrai, par d'autres. (I, **312**)

All the themes associated with Gilberte are rehearsed and re-examined in relation to Albertine: the sense of reality and dream, especially in relation to names, the physical acquaintance through games, and the socialising that centres at first on sharing food.

Taking first the importance of names, we can see that some time before his stroke of luck in meeting Albertine in Elstir's studio the narrator had happened to hear the name Simonet. When he meets Albertine he muses on the spelling of her name with its snobbish single 'n' (II, **234**) but before this the mere sound of the name had been enough to encourage him to build an imaginary world around it. Embroidering on the name links with the narrator's previous tendency over Mme de Guermantes and Gilberte to tame the unknown by creating a dream. Hearing the name Simonet in connection with the group of girls provides an exact location for his interest in them to develop. The mystery of the name is enough to trigger his old habit of wishful thinking:

> J'avais en moi de vieilles rêveries qui dataient de mon enfance et où toute la tendresse qui était dans mon cœur, mais qui éprouvée par lui ne s'en distinguait pas, m'était apportée par un être aussi différent que possible de moi. Cet être, une fois de plus je le fabriquais, en utilisant pour cela le nom de Simonet et le souvenir de l'harmonie qui régnait entre les jeunes corps que j'avais vus se déployer sur la plage, en une procession sportive digne de l'antique et de Giotto. Je ne savais pas laquelle de ces jeunes filles était Mlle Simonet, si aucune d'elles s'appelait ainsi, mais je savais que j'étais aimé de Mlle Simonet [...].
> (II, **192-3**)

The close association with Gilberte had come about either through playing games on the Champs-Élysées, including their tussle over the letter to Swann (I, **158**), or going to her 'goûters' (I, **165**). The parallels with Albertine move on to a more serious stage and emphasise the sensuality to be found in the group situation. Even as he sits on the cliff-top with the girls 'assemblées autour de moi', eating their Cheddar sandwiches and ready to play games, the narrator is carried away by the taste of 'un gâteau au chocolat gothiquement historié de sucre ou une tarte à l'abricot' to memories of Gilberte and even beyond (II, **300-301**). It is in a similar heady atmosphere of potential sensuality that physical contact is made with Albertine in the childish game of 'furet'. Proust places just before this the episode where Albertine reads out Gisèle's high-flown literary composition on Sophocles and Racine, which is followed by Andrée's cleverly severe assessment of it. The context of the crystallising of the narrator's love for Albertine is thus young people enjoying being clever, overflowing with admiration for each other, then swinging from intellectual pretension to playing childish games.

It is in the middle of Andrée's highbrow performance that Albertine slips him her little note: 'Je vous aime bien' and the atmosphere is indeed described as a still-undifferentiated cluster of erotic possibilities where the narrator feels that he is in love with' tout le groupe de ces jeunes filles, pris dans l'ensemble de ces après-midi sur la falaise' (II, 312-13). What makes the narrator decide on Albertine is the game of 'furet' with the passing of the ring and the feel of her hands, not the long-fingered elegant hands of Andrée that had provided Elstir with a perfect study but those plumper, sensual hands that went so well with Albertine's rosy complexion (II, 316-19). Even at this point Proust reminds us of the parallel to be drawn between Albertine and Gilberte. As the narrator leaves the game he catches sight in a nearby dell of 'un buisson d'aubépines défleuries' (II, 320) that brings back to him not only the childhood scenes of the hawthorns in Combray, but also the moment he met Gilberte for the first time precisely in that sensual atmosphere of the hawthorn blossom. The reader may recall at the words 'comme Gilberte avait été mon premier amour pour une jeune fille' the strange detail of her 'geste indécent' (*Swann*, 250) and become aware of a sad undernote in what on the surface appears a mere whiff of nostalgia. With a little hindsight we are alerted to the steel-like structures behind what is deceptively flimsy. As an instance of what Proust meant by claiming that his work in general was indeed planned and not a 'salade', there is, in the same context, the moment when the narrator goes away from the group with Andrée and says nice things about Albertine to her. The narrator's incidental comment looks well ahead and provides the hint, even at this point of innocent adolescent joy, of darker associations that will later trouble his mind as he learns of Albertine's sexual preferences:'... mes compliments à l'adresse de son amie n'avaient pas l'air de lui faire plaisir' (II, 319).

The final part gradually moves towards closer physical contact with Albertine now that the narrator has clearly singled her out from her friends. He has to move from the socializing of the group to the test of a one-to-one relationship. As happened with Gilberte, he will discover that the problem turns on the all-or-nothing possession of the other. A certain narrative tension is created: will he or won't he succeed? His biggest obstacle is that as he proceeds further in getting to know Albertine he becomes more and more aware of her elusiveness, and the closer he gets to the reality of Albertine the further that reality recedes. The greatest sense of the impossibility of truly knowing Albertine emerges in the moment when, invited by her to come to her room at the hotel, he attempts to kiss her and is strongly rebuffed (II, 333). Possession of the other is not as simple a matter as he thought. Even though he reacts by considering whether to flirt with Andrée on the rebound from his thwarted expectations, he discovers that he returns to Albertine, resigning himself to her complex variability. As the holiday finishes and the girls depart the narrator is prepared to be left behind and accept the melancholy conclusion to what had promised to be exciting discoveries, which now fade like the end of summer. *Nom de pays: le pays* ends with the same mixture of regret and hope to be found after the narrator's exhilaration and sadness over Gilberte in *Autour de Mme Swann*.

Chapter Three

Characterisation

Jeunes filles is remarkable for the extent to which certain principles and practices of character presentation are established. These involve both the practical novelistic technique of when and how to introduce a character, so as to maintain the reader's interest, and also a way of looking at what people are, how they perceive others and are in turn perceived. Proust is interested in his characters not only for the part they have in the narrative, but also for the unfolding of a philosophy of human relationships. Novelists have always been faced with the twin problems of describing characters and of inviting us to judge them as if they were real people about whom, it is tacitly agreed, we have been adequately informed. Everything turns on the manner of informing. In *Jeunes filles,* Proust brings to a head what this problem means for him and in that respect we see how it is a part of his originality to write obsessively about the problem of informing the reader. In so doing he contributes to the revolution in the relationship of writer and reader which has become a characteristic of modern literature.

The problems have generally been resolved by the demands of story-telling and by the omniscient stance taken by the novelist. The emphasis has usually been on an objectification of the character about whom the reader assumes that someone—the novelist as God in his own universe—knows all there is to know. It is assumed that the novelist can be trusted to reveal to the reader, at certain strategic moments, what is necessary for plot or suspense. This control is primarily exercised in the name of efficiently managing the economy of the novel as a narrative in which the yarn, or story-telling element, must go relentlessly to a conclusion. This is so even in those cases where the story-line is deliberately banal and the emphasis is on character study since, as the common reader readily acknowledges, the story cannot be held back while the narrator examines for several pages the significance of an attitude, a gesture, or a mere look. Even less acceptable is a narrator who questions whether his information is correct and admits that his previous assumptions about a character have been destabilised. The reader's expectation is that the novelist should know what he or she is about, and should use the novel to explicate it rather than spread doubt about whether anyone can be really sure of the truth of the characters presented.

Proust, as avid reader, was brought up on these assumptions and accepted them in novels he enjoyed and felt completely at ease with, novels not only by Balzac, Flaubert and Zola in the French realist vein, but also by George Eliot, Hardy and Dickens. However, as a creator himself, while he clearly took inspiration from realist techniques, he followed nevertheless his own genius which moved naturally towards a modification, if not at first outright rejection, of the assumptions of both realism and omniscience. A novelist must perforce describe people, and to follow Proust's development in his descriptions from his first short stories in *Les Plaisirs et les Jours,* through some of the sketches of *Jean Santeuil* and on through *Swann* is to see the evolution towards a philosophy of how people can be perceived, which is to emerge most clearly in the approaches to character presentation he uses in *Jeunes filles.* Thereafter, these hold good for the remainder of *La Recherche* and can be seen culminating in the pastiche of the style of the Goncourt brothers in *Le Temps retrouvé,* which categorically rejects the limitations of a realist technique because it can only record at best the surface of things and people. What the narrator at that point in the novel discovers is that his method of psychological analysis in depth is a far more rewarding method. His ability not merely to observe people, but to x-ray them, holds out to him the hope that he will have thereby the originality that a true creator must have. Proust, of course, as instigator of the whole venture has come to these views before starting out on the search for a vocation that constitutes *La Recherche,* but his narrator, who can be thought of as not being Proust himself but a creation in his own right, is shown not only gradually discovering the fauna in the world around him, but also examining his understanding of each animal both in its habitat and at different moments in its evolution. The emphasis for Proust is less on people as fixed states and more on the change that must result from seeing the same material from a different perspective in time, or from a new angle. He maintains the illusion that the narrator is relatively naïve until the final realisation in *Le Temps retrouvé* of how the subject of his work of art will indeed be both his encounter with the world and the place of his sensibility in it. What is especially interesting for both the narrator's coming to terms with people and Proust's managing of the illusion of discovery is that it is in *Jeunes filles* that he finds the ideal place for these fundamental human and aesthetic revelations through the simple device of linking them precisely with the tender, impressionable and urgent period of adolescence. It is the callow nature of the narrator's awareness of Swann, Saint-Loup, Charlus, Elstir, and above all Albertine that produces the charm of *Jeunes filles* by emphasising the newness of experience and the touching and slighly ridiculous vulnerability of the narrator. There is no better conjuncture for learning about life than adolescence, partaking as it does of the naïveté of childhood and the almost arrogant assertiveness of first maturity. Proust's greatest quality in *Jeunes filles* is his ability to capture this state of becoming, of evolution, yet it is an evolution not only presented with the freshness of actuality—much as one might expect in a realist writer—but with the complicating comments of the older self, so that the statement of what transpires is less important than the constant reassessing of its value and its deeper, usually sadder, meaning.

Character presentation before *Jeunes filles*

When *Swann* appeared in 1913 and then *Jeunes filles* in 1919, it could have seemed that Proust had sprung Minerva-like, as a fully formed consummate master, on the stage of literature. This was not the case, for there were apprentice years, though they were little known or appreciated. His contemporaries could only have known him, if at all, as the author of a handful of short stories from the 1890s published in *Les Plaisirs et les Jours* in 1896. This was only reisssued in 1924 after the award of the Prix Goncourt, and for a long time, until the posthumous *Jean Santeuil* in 1952 and *Contre Sainte-Beuve* in 1954, there was nothing of Proust's to compare with *La Recherche.*

What these short stories in *Les Plaisirs et les Jours* do in fact show is not only the germ of many stylistic features and themes but particularly a way of looking at people and presenting characters that suggests the beginnings of those original observations in *Swann* and, especially, *Jeunes filles.* These early stories reveal that Proust's interest is not in presenting the actions of his characters dramatically from the outside as a string of adventures, or even in presenting them as self-contained portraits. His approach is subjective for all that the stories are, with one exception, told in the third person. His method is to get inside his characters and illuminate the changes in their state of mind, their actions being secondary to their reactions to their situations and experiences. Freed from the obligations of dramatic plausibility, Proust is able to put the emphasis on their psychological inner landscape by developing them in time. Both Baldassare and his nephew Alexis in 'La Mort de Baldassare Silvande' evolve in this way. At first the boy is unwilling to believe

that his uncle will die, but only a year passes and he discovers that
his concern has turned into indifference. Baldassare, in his illness,
imagines saying farewell to Oliviane but when she calls he refuses to
see her. Over the period of his reverie the picture of her in his
mental landscape has been transformed: 'elle ne lui était plus rien'.
The gulf that time puts between Mme de Breyves and M. de Laléande
in 'La Mélancolique Villégiature de Mme de Breyves' convinces her
not only of his absence and inaccessibility, but finally of 'la réalité de
son amour'. Honoré, in 'La Fin de la jalousie', gradually passes from
confidence in his love for his mistress to tormenting and debilitating
doubt on hearing rumours that she has been unfaithful to him.
Violante, in 'Violante ou la mondanité', proposes going to a foreign
court to join in the social whirl, confident that she can control her
future. She becomes aware of the replacement of her enthusiasm by
boredom. Her old tutor Augustin warns her of what time may do to
the strength of human will:

> Je reviendrai [...] vivre auprès de toi, mon cher. —Le pourrez-vous? dit
> Augustin. —On peut ce qu'on veut, dit Violante. —Mais vous ne
> voudrez peut-être plus la même chose, dit Augustin, parce que vous
> aurez *changé*. (p. 33; my emphasis).

In these same early stories, Proust resorts to the technique of
showing his characters as if caught in a geological landslip, where
information from different time levels is brutally juxtaposed to
provide the reader with a sudden and unexpected revelation about
parts of a character's nature that have either been taken for granted
or have gone completely unsuspected. He makes us aware that
appearances or first impressions may lead us astray, and enjoys
showing how subsequent observations, accidental meetings or chance
remarks yield second impressions that must be added to the first so
as to modify them. In 'La Confession d'une jeune fille', he combines
this technique with the voyeuristic, hidden observer subsequently
used in the scene in *Combray* where the narrator happens to catch
sight of Mlle Vinteuil and her friend, or in *Le Temps retrouvé* where
the narrator finds the all too convenient *œil de bœuf* through which
to spy on Charlus. The mother in 'La Confession d'une jeune fille'
discovers that her daughter is not as innocent as she had believed
when, by chance, she looks through the balcony window just as her
daughter is yielding herself avidly to the embraces of her lover. This
accidental discovery of a new side to her daughter's character,
bringing with it the revelation of what she is really like, requires
such an adjustment in her understanding that it kills her. Honoré,
too, in 'La Fin de la jalousie' resorts to the technique of the voyeur
when he considers investigating the secret life of his mistress by

hiding in a bedroom to see what she is up to.

Proust's contrasting of different moments in the life of a character becomes bolder in *Jean Santeuil* and *Contre Sainte-Beuve,* and reaches its full flowering in *La Recherche.* The process has been described as 'that multilateral approach the effect of which is to lend to his great creations not only volume but the appearance of developing before one's eyes. [...] The business of the novelist [...] is to present characters in such a way as to reveal [those] complexities and obstacles which prevent one individual from knowing the true personality of another. The novelist must observe and project his characters at various descending levels of their *moi* and from different angles' (Green, pp. 15-16; cf. also p. 162). The rich harvest of this method is the panoramic treatment of characters in *La Recherche,* where a system of cross-references develops a wide-ranging network of interlocking tentacles.

In *Jean Santeuil,* which was Proust's first attempt at handling a huge field of characters, the technique has moved on from the simpler instances of the short stories and shows him becoming aware of complexity of character, not only within itself but especially in relation to a set of people who may interlock and thereby illuminate facets of each other by throwing out those interconnections that suggest not a random mass of individuals, but a community, a little world. A sense of the evolution of a character comes, for instance, through Servais, the young medical student. As the carefree drinker of champagne, with thoughts only for his own pleasure, he is contrasted with the other side of his nature when he becomes the extremely attentive doctor with a sympathetic bedside manner and the desire to put his patient before everything else. The displeasure Jean had felt earlier for the way Servais had seemed indifferent to a dying patient is replaced by the profoundest admiration. The process can be seen in M. Santeuil, a more important character. The completion of the effect of time on him comes in his late years and reveals a thorough change of attitude. The M. Santeuil who had dealt impatiently with Jean, scolding him sharply for the way he was wasting his youth, becomes a very mellow old man, now more attentive to his wife and more capable of sensitive expressions of emotion: 'M. Santeuil avait perdu peu à peu sa dureté ironique'. There are similar evolutions in Rustinlor, the *maître d'études,* who abandons his enthusiasm for poetry and develops into a banal socialite, and in Perrotin, who seems at first to be nothing more than superficial and facetious. It is only when Jean discovers that he is dying of cancer that he senses a depth to him that he had not suspected: 'On disait que Perrotin [...] avait un cancer. Et cela étonnait presque Jean, donnant à Perrotin une sorte de profondeur qu'on ne lui aurait pas cru, comme s'il lui avait découvert une vie intérieure'. *Jean Santeuil* is also instructive as a revelation of the preliminary nature of Proust's ideas of character presentation when we see how on occasion he fails to carry his technique to its full extent. If we look, for instance, at his handling of the Duc and Duchesse de Réveillon then, considering that the reader meets them frequently and at various times over a long period, there is little modification in the perception of them. The claim that the reader is fully acquainted with the Duc de Réveillon—'maintenant que vous le connaissez bien'—is not justified.

As for the multilateral approach to character presentation, this is much less tentative. The novelist C, whom the two friends meet at Kerengrimen, is to them 'fort gai, fort crotté', but he has also a more snobbish side and is 'très élégamment mis' when he goes to the local château. From another angle, C, ordinarily kind and generous, is revealed as indulging in strange, sadistic behaviour, as the two friends discover when they observe him secretly driving the lighthouse keeper's geese into the sea. The keeper and his wife suspect him of nothing. The character of Ernestine, the family servant, is described in its contradictory facets. She is very familiar in her dealings with Jean's great-aunt, with whom she gossips as they watch the passers-by, but with Jean's parents she is overly respectful. There are harder revelations behind the homely exterior of Ernestine, who could be quite nasty to the kitchen-maid working under her:

> [Jean] ignorait que soigneuse et souriante dans la salle à manger, avec les maîtres, Ernestine dans la cuisine et dans l'office, faisait pleurer la fille de cuisine, la frappant à tout propos de son ironie, de son mépris, de ses injures, de ses calomnies, jetant du poivre dans sa boisson ou des saletés dans son déjeuner [...]. (p. 282)

What *Jean Santeuil* lacks is the exploitation of these techniques to the full. If Proust's coming to terms with the complications of presenting characters is vague in *Les Plaisirs et les Jours,* it has become more affirmative in *Jean Santeuil* and finally crystallises in *Contre Sainte-Beuve,* which provides two answers to the unsatisfactoriness that may have led him, in this respect at least, to abandon his first attempt at a novel. First, he reveals in *Contre Sainte-Beuve* his admiration for Balzac's discovery of recurring characters in *La Comédie humaine,* and his disapproval of Sainte-Beuve's criticism of this method as dull. Speaking of Vautrin and Lucien de Rubempré passing the château de Rastignac and the illumination this gives of Vautrin's character, Proust remarks:

De tels effets ne sont guère possibles que grâce à cette admirable
invention de Balzac d'avoir gardé les mêmes personnages dans tous ses
romans. Ainsi un rayon détaché du fond de l'œuvre, passant sur toute
une vie, peut venir toucher, de sa lueur mélancolique et trouble, cette
gentilhommière de Dordogne et cet arrêt des deux voyageurs. [...] C'est
l'idée de génie de Balzac que Sainte-Beuve méconnaît là. Sans doute,
pourra-t-on dire, il ne l'a pas eue tout de suite. Telle partie de ses grands
cycles ne s'y est trouvée rattachée qu'après coup. Qu'importe?
L'Enchantement du vendredi saint est un morceau que Wagner écrivit
avant de penser à faire *Parsifal* et qu'il y introduisit ensuite. Mais les
ajoutages, ces beautés rapportées, les rapports nouveaux aperçus
brusquement par le génie entre les parties séparées de son œuvre qui se
rejoignent, vivent et ne pourraient plus se séparer, ne sont-ce pas de ses
plus belles intuitions? La sœur de Balzac nous a raconté la joie qu'il
éprouva le jour où il eut cette idée, et je la trouve aussi grande ainsi que
s'il l'avait eue avant de commencer son œuvre. C'est un rayon qui a
paru, qui est venu se poser à la fois sur diverses parties ternes jusque-là
de sa création, les a unies, fait vivre, illuminées, mais ce rayon n'en est
pas moins parti de sa pensée. (p. 274)

Delight in Balzac's cyclical method appears in due course in *La
Recherche*, and coupled again with Wagner, in whom he admired the
complementary nature of the operas of *The Ring*. Indeed, the point
in *La Recherche* where the narrator is conscious of the evocative
powers of the Wagnerian leitmotiv serves as a foil to the method of
character presentation that Proust himself was fully exploiting at this
time (*La Prisonnière*, **257-60**). In a comment on *La Comédie
humaine*, Proust points out that the unit in Balzac is not the novel,
because the Balzacian world would be better described as a cycle in
which a single novel is only a part. Proust derives from Balzac a
deep interest in this building up of a cycle, and especially of the
passage of time that is revealed in the course of it. By the time of
writing *Jeunes filles* he was well into the application of a technique
of setting up his characters by slow degrees and in layers, as if they
had evolved by geological accretion. This is how, in *Contre Sainte-
Beuv*, he describes his insight into reading a favourite author:

Bien montrer pour Balzac (*La Fille aux yeux d'or, La Duchesse de
Langeais*, etc.) les lentes préparations, le sujet qu'on ligote peu à peu,
puis l'étranglement foudroyant de la fin. Et aussi l'interpolation des
temps (*La Duchesse de Langeais, Sarrazine*) comme dans un terrain où
les laves d'époques différentes sont mêlés. (p. 289; my emphasis)

At the time of writing *Jean Santeuil*, Proust was reading Balzac
novel after novel. In October 1896 he wrote to his mother requesting
several books, including *Le Curé de village, Le [sic] Ménage de
garçon* (*La Rabouilleuse*), *La Vieille Fille* and *Les Chouans* (*Corr.*,
I, 144). Indeed, in *Jean Santeuil*, Jean is a Balzac reader, and one of
the two friends in the Introduction is reading *Le Curé de village*.

Proust reveals, too, his interest in the cyclical quality of *La Comédie humaine* and the building up of characters over long stretches when he attributes to the novelist C the remark that Balzac's characters succeed best when they recur from novel to novel and allow him to express his thoughts in a formula that could serve as the best possible epigraph to *La Recherche* itself:

> ... la beauté n'est pas dans un livre, elle est dans l'ensemble. Chaque roman lu séparément n'est pas bien bon, et pourtant les personnages qu'on retrouve dans tous sont vraiment très bien. (p. 199)

If from Balzac Proust had learned the advantage of both a multiplicity of characters and their evolution in time, then the second lesson learned from *Contre Sainte-Beuve* was the use of the first-person narrator. The techniques of character presentation suggested in *Les Plaisirs et les Jours* and elaborated in *Jean Santeuil* remain unsatisfactory until given a central point from which to radiate, and it is this that is given its trial run in *Contre Sainte-Beuve* before reaching its full realization with the narrator in *La Recherche*. He is someone who could be described as a relatively fixed centre, since the essence of the narrator is to be watchful of evolution even within himself and not only in those around him. To compare *Contre Sainte-Beuve* with *Jean Santeuil* is to realize that, with his first full-length fictional experiment, Proust is struggling in his use of the third-person narration to disguise his natural approach to characterisation. This false start must have been the first step towards its failure and probably why he set it aside. The use of the third person was always a pretence and an encumbrance and a momentary slipping of the mask in *Jean Santeuil* is enough to show that for Proust a sophisticated first person—recognisable without being totally confessional—is the natural means for communication. In a chapter which develops into an essay on Balzac, we find that the novelist C speaks out in his own voice on the problems of relating life and art. The use of the first person 'je' (obviously Proust himself) came so easily in these pages of theoretical speculation that in *La Recherche* the only survival of the old third-person technique is *Un amour de Swann*.

Character presentation in *Jeunes filles*

The techniques described here come together in *Jeunes filles* in two ways. They appear first as a consolidation of the methods elaborated in *Combray* and *Un amour de Swann*, then secondly, and more importantly for a novel of adolescent self-discovery, as a point of departure for a maturing narrator who is beginning to appreciate more and more deeply the strangeness of human behaviour, its potential for elusiveness, and the concomitant demand for redefinition both of the character involved and the observer.

In taking first the matter of consolidating previous views on a character's behaviour, the reader of *Jeunes filles* can appreciate with hindsight the importance given to the characterisation of Swann, especially in that part of *Combray* where the narrator begins to question the shortcomings of his great-aunt's tendency to predetermine all that Swann is and cast him in an unchanging role, when all along the real Swann was just as much the sum of the gaps in her knowledge as in the parts that were plainly apparent. In her tendency to foreclose what Swann should be she was already fleshing out a man whom the narrator perceived less solidly as 'l'obscur et incertain personnage' emerging from the shadows on his visits to his parents, and recognised mainly as a voice. Already the narrator is aware that the Swann of his childhood is not only the solid country gentleman his family sees, but a starting point for different personalities, different Swanns. Those who knew him in different circles supplied 'élégances' to fill out their creation, while his parents could take the same potential personality and fill it out with the happy occasions of their weekly dinners. In both cases Swann is described in physical terms as a territory to be taken over or as an empty container to be filled up with what those who observe him from the outside wish to put there:

> Sans doute, dans le Swann qu'ils s'étaient constitué, mes parents avaient omis par ignorance de faire entrer une foule de particularités de sa vie mondaine qui étaient cause que d'autres personnes, quand elles étaient dans sa présence, voyaient les élégances régner dans son visage et s'arrêter à son nez busqué comme à leur frontière naturelle; mais aussi ils avaient pu entasser dans ce visage désaffecté de son prestige, vacant et spacieux, au fond de ces yeux dépréciés, le vague et doux résidu—mi-mémoire, mi-oubli—des heures oisives passées ensemble après nos dîners hebdomadaires, autour de la table de jeu ou au jardin, durant notre vie de bon voisinage campagnard. (*Swann*, 113)

In *Un amour de Swann,* the narrator will reveal the very opposite of the bland visitor of *Combray.* Swann is shown to be the victim of his self-indulgent nature, caught out in his pursuit of women by a woman who was not his 'genre' (*Swann*, 521); he is, in fact, the prey of her duplicity. In addition, his physical drive to self-assertion as elegant socialite is counterpointed by the lack of spiritual drive evident in his inability to concentrate enough on his insights into art to complete his study of Vermeer. As Proust moves into *Jeunes filles,* he consolidates this way of seeing Swann. What had been Swann observed by others becomes Swann as part of his direct experience. The narrator's sense of the evolution of Swann and the palpable feel of change in direction are at first evident in seeing Swann as the indulgent father of Gilberte. Later, by the touch on the tiller, the *coup de barre,* in *Autour de Mme Swann* the narrator becomes aware of the shift in Swann's outlook now that he has become domestically docile and socially contrite as husband of Odette.

Jeunes filles consolidates some other observations of people in *Combray.* The negative sides of Françoise (she who enjoyed killing the hens and being hard on the kitchen-maid) and of Legrandin (he of the flowery poeticism and the fleshy rump that betrayed his snobbish toadying) are tokens of the sharp adjustments that have to be made when what we wish to believe is contradicted by reality. In *Jeunes filles,* the incidental discovery that Mme de Villeparisis is related to the Guermantes transforms her from the lady who presented the narrator with a box of chocolates as a child into someone of a more elevated status. In his childhood she had had no special standing, but now 'subissait brusquement une de ces hausses fantastiques' (II, **134**) and partakes of 'des changements aussi nombreux que les métamorphoses d'Ovide' (*ibid*). We are likewise prepared for adjustments to the narrator's knowledge of Gilberte, who may not be the innocent girl of the narrator's calf-love but a budding bisexual, and for adjustments in the case of Albertine, whose very elusiveness in this part of the novel is itself a preparation for the secret life the narrator will be shattered to discover after her death. The volte-face element suggested in *Combray* grows stronger in *Jeunes filles.* It lurks beneath the innocent surface only to emerge in later parts of *La Recherche* as a very pessimistic view of the evolution of people.

Alongside these observations of people we find in *Jeunes filles* that Proust is harnessing all those discoveries from the time of his first short stories onwards—subjectivism, the discrepancies between the real and the imagined, the evolution of characters in time and the continual modifications to be made in our knowledge of others—in a way that throws the development of the narrator into sharper relief than in the childhood section of *Combray.* There the lessons of adjustment have a sense of being reported; in *Jeunes filles* there is a feeling of the narrator's evolution in action. This is conveyed almost palpably by his discovery of those shifts in viewpoint that happen to him directly and cause him to look inward. We see as part of his immediate experience what had previously only been demonstrated to him at a remove. Proust breaks new ground, particularly by confronting the narrator in sequence with Norpois, Saint-Loup, Charlus, Elstir and Albertine. Where previously he had explained behaviour, and the significance of the way in which it was understood, in a discursive style, with *Jeunes filles* he proceeds more by a dramatic method and presents new attitudes with less elaborate comment, allowing the incidents to speak largely for themselves. He brings out what is important by letting us watch the narrator experience directly, so that we bear witness to his confused and innocent view of the world. This feeling of a quickening in the narrator's progress and of an immediacy of experience is traceable even in *Noms de pays: le nom*. This is the first time in *La Recherche* that we see the narrator *en situation* and obliged to make decisions, viz. his encounters with Gilberte, his discovery of his dependence on her and his losing her. Compared with *Combray,* this involves both action and reflection, whereas in *Combray* we are only aware of the narrator's observation of the world around him, his sensitive reactions, the people he comes acrosss and their emblematic roles, such as kind / cruel Françoise, or snobbish Legrandin. Once involved with Gilberte, however, the narrator has to come to terms with another individual and perforce to face up to a world of interaction with others rather than resign himself to the passive observation of them. We observe him in the throes of a relationship which he fails to control. Losing Gilberte, he discovers, is part of the difficulty of living, which becomes for him the problem of balancing his own world of feelings against the obligations of commitment that the other requires. When he eventually meets Saint-Loup and Albertine, this problem of the equality of value in encountering another personality with whom to share friendship will be simply the extending of the experience he has already gone through in *Noms de pays: le nom* with Gilberte. Both the narrator and Gilberte begin to fill out as real people instead of being the shadowy presences they are in *Combray,* the narrator in particular is more convincing in a complex way from this point onwards as we slip from older man to adolescent than in *Combray* from older man to child. In terms of the strategy of character presentation there is a further filling out of the narrator, as he discovers in Swann a new dimension as father of Gilberte; in *Autour de Mme Swann,* his awareness that Swann is now glad to have almost anyone come to his wife's salon adds both to the portrayal of Swann and completes that lesson about the variability of a character's situation that had started with the family's wilful misreading of the signals given out by their country visitor. That first sketch in *Combray* of Swann as the very model of how a person cannot be fully known now comes strongly into the direct experience of the narrator, and enlightens him not only about Swann, but about

Dr Cottard's hidden qualities as well. The narrator learns to accept the whole spectrum of change that can be a mixture of gradual evolution or complete reversal:

> ... en ce qui concerne l'ensemble de façons que le professeur Cottard montrait à un homme comme mon père, remarquons que la nature que nous faisons paraître dans la seconde partie de notre vie, n'est pas toujours, si elle l'est souvent, notre nature première développée ou flétrie, grossie ou atténuée; elle est quelquefois une nature inverse, un véritable vêtement retourné. (I, **88**)

Following on from the lesson of Swann, the narrator meets Norpois and experiences at first hand yet again that obfuscation of true feelings that had been launched in *Combray* with Legrandin. Norpois is the extension into the adolescent's experience of the bumbling phoneyness caricatured in the description of the behaviour and language of Legrandin. As the narrator is shown becoming aware of the grandiloquence of Norpois, however, there is more to it than creating distance through caricature. There could be something to learn, and the adolescent mind is in fact particularly suited to seeing the ridiculous but also to being flexible enough to change. Legrandin in *Combray* is seen by the narrator as the family sees him, viz. as a snob whom they try to catch out over his connections in Balbec (*Swann*, **238-9**). Norpois, in *Jeunes filles*, also allowed like Legrandin plenty of verbal rope to hang himself, impinges directly on the narrator and is seen by him to be an obstacle to his dreams and expectations, at first encouraging him to write and then coldly disregarding his modest efforts. Comparing the language of Legrandin and Norpois shows how much more dramatically involved the narrator is with Norpois, who, in his verbal dexterity, oozes confidence and a sense of control of the world about him. He shares to some extent the ludicrous logorrhoea of Legrandin's literary posturing and simpering (*Swann*, **226-7**) but in Legrandin's case the exaggeration in presenting him distances him from the narrator and makes him merely a figure of fun:

> «Venez tenir compagnie à votre vieil ami, m'avait-il dit. [...] Venez avec la primevère, la barbe de chanoine, le bassin d'or, venez avec le sedum dont est fait le bouquet de dilection de la flore balzacienne, avec la fleur du jour de la Résurrection, la pâquerette et la boule de neige des jardins qui commence à embaumer dans les allées de votre grand-tante quand ne sont pas encore fondues les dernières boules de neige des giboulées de Pâques. Venez avec la glorieuse vêture de soie du lis digne de Salomon [...]». (*Swann*, **233**)

This is very much Legrandin from the outside. With Norpois, however, there is a feeling that the narrator is not simply gawping at a caricature, but finding someone with whom he has to interact and whose contorted advice he is not absolutely sure how to take. He realises that his efforts to widen his horizons, whether in admiring La Berma's performance in *Phèdre* or submitting his literary creations to Norpois for an opinion, have to be put into perspective in relation to the judgements Norpois has in store. His *petit poème en prose,* for instance, fails to impress, and this for the moment at least checks his advance. Though nonplussed on the literary front by his enigmatic remarks, he finds unexpected help in the view Norpois provides on La Berma, which makes the narrator appreciate that his preconceived wish for a flamboyant performance from the celebrated actress was to do with theatricalism and not art. Norpois shows him that the artist in La Berma concentrates energy and does not dissipate it in unnecessary projection, and least of all, in excessive gesture. The confrontation with Norpois makes the narrator reflect and reappraise his position. Above all he tempers his views of creativity—his own as well as La Berma's—by paralleling his inexperience with Norpois and his worldly wisdom. When Norpois speaks he is only in part a caricature of a man high on pomposity. There is also for the narrator a lesson to be learnt from going beyond the wind-bag side of Norpois, the verbally clever diplomat, to the shrewdness of a man trained to temper extravagance. The narrator's position regarding Norpois is revised precisely by his having to take the opinions of Norpois on board and modify his own view of La Berma. In addition, the adolescent is changed from a naïve stance to a more sophisticated one, and a stance, moreover, which becomes part of his education in aesthetics. The words of Norpois ring in the narrator's ears until he gets the message of adjustment and thereby of making spiritual progress:

> «Jamais de couleurs trop voyantes, de cris exagérés. Et puis cette voix admirable qui la sert si bien et dont elle joue à ravir, je serais presque tenté de dire en musicienne!» [...]
> «C'est vrai, me disais-je, quelle belle voix, quelle absence de cris, quels costumes simples, quelle intelligence d'avoir été choisir *Phèdre.* Non, je n'ai pas été déçu!». (I, **116**)

What the narrator loses on the matter of literature—'Jusqu'ici je m'étais seulement rendu compte que je n'avais pas le don d'écrire; maintenant M. de Norpois m'en ôtait même le désir' (I, **110**)—he gains in his understanding of craft versus art, in that as La Berma controls the potential exhibitionism that lies in the craft and technique of acting, she increases her submission to her subject and thereby the impact of her creative insight, her art. The ambiguous guide Norpois, whose froth of words nevertheless can on occasion hide perceptiveness, leads the narrator to a true guide, La Berma. Her art leads in turn to clarifying the progress to be made in his vocation.

A further step in the idea of the artist's devotion to his or her art, above personal vanity and even above dedicating oneself to other people, emerges in the narrator's acquaintance with Saint-Loup. Having heard about him from his aunt, Mme de Villeparisis, the narrator is excited to think that they will have a lot in common and be good friends from the word go. However, he is disappointed on actually meeting him to find him at first almost rudely indifferent. It transpires that this aloofness is only a superficial characteristic. Saint-Loup's real nature is warm and relaxed, so much so that the narrator finds in him 'un autre être bien différent de celui que je soupçonnais' (II, **109**). The adolescent's first experience of Saint-Loup is that need to adjust to the real person behind the public façade, which in this case conceals an aristocrat who is not at all typical of his class and is proud of his intellectual and advanced liberal views. It is, however, precisely this change in stance that, while bringing the two together, makes the narrator suddenly aware of a need within him to keep his distance. Ironically, at the moment when he should be receiving the gift of mutual friendship, he realizes that he regrets spending time with Saint-Loup which he should be devoting to applying whatever talent he has for creative work. He speaks strongly of cutting himself off from others, as if not to do so would be to miss the crucial moment that could at last allow him to move forward after the check to his ambitions he had encountered with Norpois. He detects 'une sorte de remords, de regret, de fatigue de ne pas être resté seul et prêt enfin à travailler' (II, **113**). He finds himself seeing in Saint-Loup 'un être plus général que lui-même, le «noble»' (II, **114**). He cannot naively accept the friendship he has been offered for itself and give himself to it unreservedly, for that would be to admit the dereliction of the artist's, or potential artist's, duty to preserve the total freedom of the creator's sensibility. We are present at the dawning of a moment of self-realization that pushes the narrator's aesthetic development into a new dimension as the narrator senses this instinctive awareness of artistic duty that may allow the lesser degree of comradeship but not the complete surrender of the self that friendship requires. We are observing the narrator coming to terms with his temperamental inability to accept self-sacrifice because his budding artistic self intervenes to impose the artist's duty, specifically the duty to observe dispassionately, to seek to reveal the patterns that harmony of form demands, to keep the individual in second place in the name of the universal that art requires, and above all to preserve an intellectual distance:

Il [Saint-Loup] n'était plus qu'un objet que ma rêverie cherchait à approfondir. A retrouver toujours en lui cet être antérieur, séculaire, cet aristocrate que Robert aspirait justement à ne pas être, j'éprouvais une vive joie, mais d'intelligence, non d'amitié. [...] Quelquefois je me reprochais de prendre ainsi plaisir à considérer mon ami comme une œuvre d'art, c'est-à-dire à regarder le jeu de toutes les parties de son être comme harmonieusement réglé par une idée générale à laquelle elles étaient suspendues mais qu'il ne connaissait pas et qui par conséquent n'ajoutait rien à ses qualités propres, à cette valeur personnelle d'intelligence et de moralité à quoi il attachait tant de prix. (*ibid*)

A similar view is expressed later when the narrator prefers to frequent Albertine and her friends instead of Saint-Loup. We catch him in the act of upping the importance of his inner life, especially as fuel for his ambition to become an artist. He feels that friendship, in this respect, prevents that inward communication that is the life-blood of the artist for whom 'la loi de développement est purement interne', and for whom friendship is therefore 'une abdication de soi' (II, **303**).

Against the obsession with the elaboration of the narrator's aesthetic adventure there runs parallel to it the sketching-in of the narrator's last stages of innocence before deeper cynicism takes over the freshness of adolescence for good. Shadows had lurked in *Combray,* but in *Jeunes filles* they are clearly evident to the reader even if the narrator cannot quite understand them. What the reader sees in the Charlus episode is the tinge of dramatic irony that Proust contrives so as to allow us to interpret hints that the narrator in his younger form is as yet too lacking in guile to appreciate. It is a way, once again, of letting the reader be present at the actual moment of the narrator's evolution, not referring back to an experience so much as taking us through the actual incident. We observe the narrator almost falling victim to a sexual takeover that he will only fully understand when more mature; he does not, at this point, understand the significance of what is happening or the exact interest of Charlus in making his acquaintance. The narrator is *en situation,* not reporting but almost succumbing. The shadows brush past.

The first meeting with Saint-Loup's uncle Palamède de Guermantes is a model of Proust's technique in setting up the narrator as naïve participant. It will be a preparation for other instances involving this character, notably when the narrator will, with greater insight, secretly observe the concerted ballet of mannerisms that reveal the truth about Charlus as he is engaged in another takeover bid, viz. the courtship of Jupien.

This first acquaintance falls into two stages in accordance with the narrator's previous experiences and with Proust's favoured technique of presentatation. First comes the impression centred on the name

(II, **127-8**) and on an ideal surrounding it, then the reality of an actual meeting, with consequent adjustments. This meeting parallels both Gilberte and Albertine, and even Elstir. A considerable interest is built specifically on the exotic-sounding 'Palamède' that creates around it both music and mystery. Around that name comes first important attendant information, viz. Palamède will arrive at Balbec after virtually hiking there. The picture built up in this first stage is of a butch or macho figure reinforced by his odd and aggressive behaviour, a leader of fashion in his younger years, and a womaniser and now protector of men whom he has put forward for posts or whose careers he has promoted. Without Saint-Loup's realizing it, certain strange elements seem to be integrated into the picture. Saint-Loup describes his uncle's *garçonnière,* shared with two other friends, all three known by the ambiguous nickname of «les trois Grâces». This is recalled in all innocence by Saint-Loup, who seems also to be unaware that this could be a heterosexual front, something which could be confirmed by the anecdote involving a kind of homosexual advance at the *garçonnière* that had led Palamède and his two friends to assault a visitor. Palamède's behaviour brings out a relish for violence and queer-bashing that is both disturbing at this point and premonitory. He and his friends 'prirent le coupable, le déshabillèrent et le frappèrent jusqu'au sang' (II, **129**).

The second stage brings out at first the narrator's sense of alarm at being watched by a stranger, and then his increasing interest in the secret life of Charlus once he realizes who this stranger is. At first the narrator is only aware of being an object in the laser-like beam of the stranger's gaze outside the casino, the gaze of someone who is almost on the point of giving away his secret, marauding interest in the young man. Everything about Charlus is on the brink of betraying his true nature and his real interest in this exercise of 'picking up' the narrator. The only obvious sign—which the narrator does not fully comprehend at this point—is the look. In all other respects the stranger he encounters is not giving out any signs, indeed he has dressed with exceptional elegance, but dressed down to a level of sobriety. The effect on the narrator is not what the stranger intends. There is a certain comedy in the way the narrator misreads the signs and sees not a come-on but something furtive and dangerous—the epithets he uses are *fou, espion, escroc d'hôtel, voleur* and *aliéné* (II, **131-2**).

On close examination we can see step by step the setting out of the problematic nature both of Charlus himself and of the uncomfortable way the narrator begins to learn about this mysterious person. This process is a key element in the narrator's education. Proust is playing off the enigmas (part of the essential nature of Charlus) against the way our acquisition of knowledge is piecemeal and imprecise, causing us to be trapped in dilemmas when all the time we are driven by curiosity and hanker after certainties. The whole Charlus story can be seen here in miniature, since it will take the narrator a very long time indeed to tumble to the truth about his furtiveness. It is precisely this sinister quality that increases his strangeness at the time of the narrator's adolescent encounter with him and gives direction to all his attempts at concealment.

The section dealing with Charlus (II, **127-48**), subtitled 'Premiers crayons de M. de Charlus et de Robert de Saint-Loup' (Pléiade I, 642), is itself a preparation in the narrator's learning process before he eventually meets the girls. The real nature of things is never handed to any one of us as a cut-and-dried phenomenon, but emerges as part of a process of finding out heuristically. What we call our knowledge of someone is the result of trial and error in our efforts to collect the tessera that will eventually be fitted more or less correctly into the mosaic. The example of Swann in *Combray* is the paradigm Proust had placed before us to guide us in this process of appreciating the complexity of any given individual. So here the adolescent's bewilderment with Charlus sets up yet another paradigm for the difficulty he will have in being sure he can know anyone for certain, especially Albertine. The strangeness of Charlus sets the tone for a difficulty the narrator will have generally in coming to terms with the other, and most poignantly of course in the intimacy of a sexual relationship. The relationship so far with Gilberte has alerted him to the difficulty of compatibility with another individual, and left him scarred. The encounter with the mystery of Charlus is the first time we see him discovering that the impossibility of total sureness about the other is the application to his own experience of the general idea so far illustrated through Swann and Odette. He is put on the spot, not by a notional strangeness of the other but by an instance of it that painfully leaves him in a state of doubt, the full extent of which he will only know after he meets Albertine, lives with her and—in all senses of the word—loses her. Proust has been careful to present us with this moment of dilemma before the adolescent actually meets Albertine at Balbec, thereby prefiguring the narrator's tragic experience of having to accept the secrecy of Albertine. That secrecy will be as intense, and as covert, as the impression here of the inscrutability of the gaze of Charlus, dangerously hidden like an enemy behind the arrow-slit of an impregnable fortress.

The close reading of this section, bearing in mind these approaches, reveals that game of skilful dovetailing and anticipation that gives Proust's text the almost musical richness he claimed for the whole novel. Hints of past themes and yet more precursory notes of new themes provide a texture of leitmotifs that develop in complexity and transformative power, so that nothing seems to have appeared as a one-off but everything contributes to everything else with a cumulative force, rather in the manner of Wagnerian 'symphonic opera', that Proust both admired and empathized with.

Proust exhibits in these 'premiers crayons' the importance of the manner in which information is acquired so that, though the reader may end up with a portrait of a character, there is no atttempt to provide any definitive portrait at all but rather a sequence of atomized pieces of information that may possibly be made into a whole. Proust never lays down the law that a character is this or that, but reveals how the completeness of a character can only be perceived in bits and how any concluding whole that is arrived at, no doubt temporarily, is itself a creation of the observer. Above all in *Jeunes filles,* he is making us aware that the narrator's education with regard to the understanding of people is dependent on his having to submit, as here in the case of Charlus, to this seemingly unsatisfactory atomization.

The section on Charlus ends with an incident that draws attention to Proust's frequent dramatic method in *Jeunes filles.* Placed before us, and virtually without comment, is the enigmatic arrival in the narrator's bedroom of Charlus bearing gifts—books by the narrator's favourite author, Bergotte, to help him while away his sleepless hours (II, **146-8**). Like Dickens, Proust has the gift of choosing the moment to let a character talk and reveal more of himself to the reader than the recipient is able to understand. The technique Charlus uses for this interview is—perhaps unconsciously—to play by turns Mr Nice and Mr Nasty, sometimes flowery, sometimes abrupt, and to blow up the ostensibly trivial into something portentous. It is on the surface only a matter of arranging to get the right book, but more deeply—perhaps again unconsciously—it is a playing off of older man against inexperienced youth in a sort of power tussle. The following day, when the narrator meets Charlus just before the latter is about to leave Balbec, he is subjected to an excessively matey Charlus, who with undue familiarity pinches his neck jokingly but follows it up with an enigmatic dressing down that leaves the narrator completely foxed as to how to take this bizarre blend of physical contact and verbal rudeness. This ambiguous blend of flattering attention and curt dismissal is enough to leave any adolescent, innocently seeking guidance in the ways of the world, even more confused. Unusually, Proust leaves the incident with no comment, which emphasizes not only the dramatic method, but also transmits to us the narrator's sense of bewilderment as it happens. In a dramatic situation there is no better parting than a Parthian shot: Charlus sends back the book, elevating it, since it is bound in morocco with an incised motif of forget-me-nots, to the rank of precious token.

If the Charlus episode shows the adolescent as vulnerable to the ways of the world and not yet quite ready to understand them, the meeting with Elstir and Albertine brings out specifically the moment when the narrator's thoughts about art are clarified by meeting a real artist, and his encounter with the opposite sex resolved by meeting a real girl.

The meeting with Elstir poses before the narrator the problem of public and private image, the artist and society. (The full impact of the paintings will be discussed in the following chapter.) Proust shows us, in opposing the narrator and Elstir, that this fundamental aesthetic problem is something the narrator has already had an inkling of in describing the views of Mme de Villeparisis, but that he is now on the point of resolving. Essentially, the view of Mme de Villeparisis had been inclined to bear much more on the man than on the work, emphasizing gossip at the expense of talent and reducing appreciation of a work of the imagination to the trivial (II, **96-8**). With Elstir, we see the narrator sharing the dilemma of Mme de Villeparisis but finding a new direction for himself. She is able to trivialise writers precisely because she insists on making parallels between their literary reputations and their personal visits to her family. The shortcomings of their mannerisms are enough, in her eyes, to demote the quality of their work. Gossip does not, in this case, help her to illuminate their creations but to diminish them. Thus Chateaubriand is identified with his description of moonlight and whenever he repeats it is mocked for his predictability rather than admired for his invention, especially if he can be literally led up the garden path when the moon is high and made to perform: 'M de Chateaubriand se contentait de servir toujours un même morceau tout préparé' (II, **97**). This is the view of the artist as monkey. Vigny, Musset and Balzac are less writers in her eyes than social climbers, and Hugo either stylistically wayward or politically out of line (II, **98**). This is the view of the artist as a creative force that can safely be tamed by denigration. Comparing, as the reader must, the Mme de Villeparisis view with the thoughts of the narrator encountering not only Elstir's paintings but the man himself, we see that Proust is setting up one of those turning-points in the narrator's understanding. At the same time, he is elucidating the way the reader sees a character modulation in both the adolescent and the older guide, Elstir. Progress is about to be made and is dependent, to some extent, on the narrator's apprehending a new side to Elstir which he had never suspected. He is surprised by certain personal details he unearths, but unlike Mme de Villeparisis, he does not fall into the error of confusing the man and the work to the detriment of the latter. The lesser instance of Mme de Villeparisis is something the reader encounters first so as to provide the contrast with a new and important change in the narrator's understanding of aesthetics. Artists do not, any more than other individuals, exist in a vacuum. They have private lives, but for them the creative side is a different one from the banal everyday self, and the artist's duty is to respond to this self if he is to be truly creative. The fact that there can be an embarrassing gap between the imaginative insight of a creation and the banal or even reprehensible private life of the artist is something to be understood positively, and not dismissively as Mme de Villeparisis does. Proust, in his reply to a famous questionnaire, defended the private life of the artist. While there may be all sorts of reasons for that view, the essential point he makes—the creative self is something other that the banal everyday individual—is revealed in *Jeunes filles* when the narrator visits Elstir's studio and eventually puts his exciting and revelatory experience of the paintings alongside those facts he discovers about their creator that lie outside the works of art he has been contemplating. These sublime paintings, and especially their quality of seeming to have named creation anew, have come from a man who was no less than the M. Biche of Mme Verdurin's salon. The shock of the banal is encountered again here, as it had been in meeting Bergotte and realizing how thoroughly ordinary he was, and even how petty he could be, compared with the creator of a literature the narrator had greatly enjoyed and admired. The difference now is that the narrator can accept this divergence and gain that valuable insight, denied to ladies of taste like Mme de Villeparisis, which enriches his understanding of the roles not only of art and reality, but also the relationship of artist to society.

Approaching Elstir almost in the way Mme de Villeparisis treats her stable of famous names from world literature, the narrator tries to dig into the painter's past. The discovery that the portrait of *Miss Sacripant* is indeed Odette provides him with the link that establishes Elstir as being 'le peintre ridicule et pervers, adopté jadis par les Verdurin'(II, **255**). Elstir, to his surprise, does not feel at all put in his place by this piece of investigative curiosity. He finds it irrelevant, and that is the moment when the narrator learns that for the true artist the separation must be maintained between the social self, which may be open to ridicule, and the creative self, which is the only one worthy of being admired. For Elstir all things hang together, and a former ridiculous phase has had its part to play, being but an element in the passage from one state to another. Just as

Proust had found the right moment to let Charlus talk, so here he
allows Elstir, the successful artist, to spell out the relationship of
artist to public and bring together for the narrator many aspects of
aesthetic problems that he has already suspected. For Elstir, a man is
not wise until he has passed through 'toutes les incarnations ridicules
ou odieuses qui doivent précéder cette dernière incarnation-là' (*ibid*).
In this long speech of Elstir's the narrator is presented to us at the
point of learning a particularly important lesson: the lesson of the
interior journey that puts the artist's creative and private life in
perspective and prepares for a positive and artistically fruitful
maturity. Elstir sets out a kind of credo: understanding is not a gift
but the product of effort, we journey alone, the ideal is not given but
is the result of an evolution from possibly banal and uncongenial
elements until it emerges victorious over them, what we have been
may be totally transformed but our past must not be denied for it is
evidence of the work we have subjected it to and from which the
artist extracts something that can be said to transcend it:

> «Je sais qu'il y a des jeunes gens, fils et petits-fils d'hommes
> distingués, à qui leurs précepteurs ont enseigné la noblesse de l'esprit et
> l'élégance morale dès le collège. Ils n'ont peut-être rien à retrancher de
> leur vie, ils pourraient publier et signer tout ce qu'ils ont dit, mais ce
> sont de pauvres esprits, descendants sans force de doctrinaires, et de qui
> la sagesse est négative et stérile. On ne reçoit pas la sagesse, il faut la
> découvrir soi-même, après un trajet que personne ne peut faire pour
> nous, ne peut nous épargner, car elle est un point de vue sur les choses.
> Les vies que vous admirez, les attitudes que vous trouvez nobles n'ont
> pas été disposées par le père de famille ou par le précepteur, elles ont été
> précédées de débuts bien différents, ayant été influencées par ce qui
> régnait autour d'elles de mal ou de banalité. Elles représentent un
> combat et une victoire. Je comprends que l'image de ce que nous avons
> été dans une période première ne soit plus reconnaissable et soit en tout
> cas déplaisante. Elle ne doit pas être reniée pourtant, car elle est un
> témoignage que nous avons vraiment vécu, que c'est selon les lois de la
> vie et de l'esprit, que nous avons, des éléments communs de la vie, de
> la vie des ateliers, des coteries artistiques s'il s'agit d'un peintre, extrait
> quelque chose qui les dépasse.» (II, **255-6**)

Of all the characters in this part of *La Recherche* whom the
narrator is aware of as evolving, and in turn making him conscious
that he himself is evolving, Albertine stands out. The quality that
attracts him to her is her changeableness, and it is this that essentially
informs the finale of *Jeunes filles*. In *La Prisonnière* and *La
Fugitive* she will be the medium whereby the narrator finally realises
the erosion of time, so much so that she will be described as 'une
grande déesse du Temps' (*La Prisonnière*, **497**; cf. also Black, p.
186). She was intended to be the linchpin, in terms of character, of
the last stages leading up to the narrator's discovery of his vocation

and it was in this vein that Proust wrote at length to Mme Scheikévitch in 1915, sketching in the broad lines of the evolution of his characters and singling out Albertine for her dramatic importance as the one who plays 'le plus grand rôle et amène la péripétie' (*Corr.*, XIV, 281).

The narrator's first impression of the elusiveness of Albertine, summed up in the phrase: 'la bacchante à bicyclette, la muse orgiaque du golf' (II, **266**), has to be fine-tuned to accommodate also the Mlle Simonet 'en robe de soie' whose long flowing hair had previously been hidden under her polo cap (II, **263**). These changes contribute to what is the 'première métamorphose' of many. The emotional charge of the narrator's interest in Albertine causes him to discover not, as he might have expected, the fixity of the object he has set his heart on, but its variability. Albertine oscillates between ordinariness and mystery to such an extent that he can conclude whimsically that he is tricked by memory as to where exactly Albertine's beauty spot is on her face:

> En face de la médiocre et touchante Albertine à qui j'avais parlé, je voyais la mystérieuse Albertine en face de la mer. C'était maintenant des souvenirs, c'est-à-dire des tableaux dont l'un ne me semblait pas plus vrai que l'autre. Pour en finir avec ce premier soir de présentation, en cherchant à revoir ce petit grain de beauté sur la joue au-dessous de l'œil, je me rappelai que de chez Elstir quand Albertine était partie, j'avais vu ce grain de beauté sur le menton. En somme, quand je la voyais, je remarquais qu'elle avait un grain de beauté, mais ma mémoire errante le promenait ensuite sur la figure d'Albertine et le plaçait tantôt ici tantôt là. (II, **268-9**)

Meeting Albertine is not something straightforward, for not only is there the overlay of the Gilberte experience, there is also the feeling that Albertine inherently represents in the narrator's mind a pull between reason—which questions whether he should get involved with her at all—and the subconscious desire to do precisely that. Whatever his 'sensibilité' or his 'intelligence' decide, his deepest wish is to meet Albertine, and it is this subconscious force that finds him instructing the coachman to drive him to Elstir's, where a little reception has been arranged. Proust takes care to establish that the link is at this elemental level (II, **262-3**). Their association, however, is very much a flesh and blood situation and it is here that the confrontation of personalities lies. Proust clearly establishes the contrast between these twin facets of ideal and real. Albertine is in part elevated symbol associated with the sea and all its variability, and in part shares the bathos of the everyday as the chubby girl with tomboyish manners and nasal twang. On one level Albertine will remain in the narrator's consciousness as essentially a disembodied force of nature, for even when he remembers her in *Le Temps retrouvé* (**234**), she is to him the essence of change and freedom: 'Albertine. foulant le sable ce premier soir, indifférente à tous, et marine, comme une mouette'. She is also in *Jeunes filles* evoked in all her immediacy as 'désirable', and humorously described with down-to-earth realism:

> En parlant, Albertine gardait la tête immobile, les narines serrées, ne faisait remuer que le bout des lèvres. Il en résultait ainsi un son traînard et nasal dans la composition duquel entraient peut-être des hérédités provinciales, une affectation juvénile de flegme britannique, les leçons d'une institutrice étrangère, et une hypertrophie congestive de la muqueuse du nez. Cette émission, qui cédait bien vite du reste quand elle connaissait plus les gens et redevenait naturellement enfantine, aurait pu passer pour désagréable. Mais elle était particulière et m'enchantait.
> (II, **270**)

His image of Albertine evolves by substituting new facets for old. This is true not only of her beauty spot or her clothes, but also of her racy manner of speaking and her abrupt, prejudiced judgements of acquaintances like Octave, dismissed as a gigolo, or Bloch, as a Yid (II, **273-4**). There are also the slangy descriptions of the local worthies (II, **276**). Albertine is the culmination of the theme of the perception of the other as a multiplicity of facets. This is not a simplistic fixing of a character in a once-only portrait, but the acceptance of an evolution in time. This had been launched with the paradigm of Swann in the opening pages of *Combray* (*Swann,* **113**). Our knowledge of the other is not a single snapshot but a set of snapshots in a whole series that is characterized by their differences. The novelty is a continuous challenge to our knowledge. Unlike the narrator's awareness of this in his impressions of Mme de Guermantes, Gilberte, or any of the characters presented so far, the Albertine experience reverses the idea of an essence. Acquaintance modifies assumptions. With Albertine, the narrator is observing the actual process of becoming aware of Albertine existentially. He senses the various possibilities appearing like a sheaf of separate and rapidly replaced images experienced in time as both subsequent and different. Referring to his perception of the girls in general he emphasizes this existential moment that is repeated in a chain of separate instances each time he confronts them. Since he is not yet 'blasé par l'habitude', he is aware of the freshness of really seeing what the other is, of experiencing each time 'un étonnement profond' (II, **313**). He is discovering in these moments that he can watch himself observing people, which leads him to put forward a new philosophy of what constitutes both our own personality and the personality of the other. He distinguishes the knowledge we have of

the other, which derives from comparing memories and reality,
from the immediacy of the evolution of the other when we are
actually face to face:

> Et cet étonnement inévitable n'est pas le seul; car à côté de celui-là il y
> en a un autre, né de la différence, non plus entre les stylisations du
> souvenir et la réalité, mais entre l'être que nous avons vu la dernière fois
> et celui qui nous apparaît aujourd'hui sous un autre angle, nous
> montrant un nouvel aspect. Le visage humain est vraiment comme celui
> du Dieu d'une théogonie orientale, toute une grappe de visages
> juxtaposés dans des plans différents et qu'on ne voit pas à la fois. (II,
> **314**)

The attitude the narrator invokes here in relation to our
perception of others provides on every occasion of his frequenting
the girls 'un violent coup de barre à mes pensées' (*ibid*), a phrase
which, while emphasising the actual moment when his mental
adjustments have to be made, recalls also the general pattern of the
modification of knowledge that he presented at the beginning of
Autour de Mme Swann regarding his ideas of both Swann and
Cottard. Proust launches in this connection a preparatory feature of
Albertine. This is her system of more or less charming duplicity,
whereby a circumstance can be exploited for its equivocal
possibilities: 'le système de fins multiples' which she shares with the
wily Norpois (II, **337-40**). This particular trait of Albertine's is
presented here by the narrator with knowledge of an Albertine well
into the future. At the time of his second visit to Balbec, in *Sodome
et Gomorrhe,* the girls are no longer the innocents of *Jeunes filles*
but sophisticated pleasure-seekers. A number of observations will
oblige the narrator to revise his view of Albertine: Cottard points
out Andrée and Albertine in the casino at Incarville dancing bust to
bust; Albertine invents excuses to get away and is so thwarted that
there is a quarrel in which she threatens to throw herself into the sea
(like Sappho, says the narrator, which comes too near to the truth);
he catches sight of Andrée nuzzling Albertine's neck with the
consequence that he is reminded of the way Albertine once behaved
strangely with Gisèle, causing the whole of the Swann / Odette
jealousy story to attach itself to his own case. The result is that he is
tormented to think what Albertine may be doing behind his back.
Her duplicity sets up connections both with her elusiveness at the
time of the first visit to Balbec and with her determination to go her
own way in *La Prisonnière* and *La Fugitive*. The moment of the
failed kiss at the Grand-Hôtel becomes a token of the future failure
of their association. Another instance of a kiss refused, which
confirms this alienation, recurs just before Albertine leaves the
narrator for good (*La Prisonnière*, **510-12**). Albertine's unexpected

detachment from the narrator will be the most 'violent coup de barre' in all his personal relationships. It is interesting to note that the narrator's experience of Albertine in *Jeunes filles* always demands an effort from him to keep all his perceptions of her together. He has to remind himself constantly about what she looks like. Not having seen her for a little while, when he sees her again and looks afresh at her features he has to go through a process of reconstituting what she is: 'sortant de la poussière du souvenir, Albertine se reconstruisait devant moi' (II, **328**).

It is her very changeability that clinches for the narrator the connection between presenting Albertine's character and realizing the evolution of his own:

> C'est peut-être parce qu'étaient si divers les êtres que je contemplais en elle à cette époque que plus tard *je pris l'habitude de devenir moi-même un personnage autre* selon celle des Albertine à laquelle je pensais: un jaloux, un indifférent, un voluptueux, un mélancolique, un furieux, recréés non seulement au hasard du souvenir qui renaissait, mais selon la force de la croyance interposée, pour un même souvenir, par la façon différente dont je l'appréciais. (II, **348**; my emphasis)

Through the interaction of the narrator with Albertine, Proust not only rounds off in *Jeunes filles* the manner in which the narrator appreciates the richness and multiplicity of his own nature, but provides as well a compendium of all those techniques of character presentation that had begun with his first short stories.

Chapter Four

Metamorphosis

Time and the ineluctable flux of change are the forces that drive *La Recherche* and dominate each of its seven parts. Memory, which is either seen as the deliberate accessing of time past or as the gratuitous revelation of it, is strongly in evidence in *Combray*, with the *madeleine* episode, and in *Un amour de Swann*, with Swann's associations of Odette and music. It is much less so in *Jeunes filles*, which, compared with all that precedes it, is primarily a study of change, catching the impressionability and malleability of adolescence in full flight as events produce their modifications of understanding and behaviour.

There is, however, in *Jeunes filles* an incident where the phenomenon of memory is given prominence. This is the moment early in Part Two when, driving along with Mme de Villeparisis, the narrator catches sight of the three trees at Hudimesnil (II, **91-4**). It is linked, since in *La Recherche* all things ultimately interconnect, with both the sense of change in the adolescent and the narrator's urgent desire to equate the most magic moments of inner examination with a justification of his past, and even of existence itself, in a search for 'une vraie vie' (II, **92**). This incident is strategically placed so that the reader can look back to the narrator's tentative literary realisation of his joy in seeing the Martinvilie steeples in *Combray*, and forward to what he is to discover as a genuine artistic achievement when he becomes acquainted with Elstir's paintings. Set against his little effort—putting his joy in the mysterious secret that the steeples held for him into words—there will be the actual realisation by a real artist of what to such an artist is 'une vraie vie'. Elstir, moreover, will demonstrate not only its overwhelming spiritual importance but also provide a method whereby to achieve it. The incident of the three trees, in showing the narrator struggling and failing to make sense of his feelings, prepares him, and the reader too, for the only possible resolution of such dilemmas, namely, not simply to record them but imaginatively to recreate them through a process of metamorphosis. In the spontaneous piece of writing about the Martinville steeples the narrator had achieved a certain elementary triumph. When he encounters Elstir and his paintings he realises that the artist has not been merely decorative but has, in recreating reality, fitted it in to his vision, thus combining his creative urge with his way of understanding the world around him and causing his expression of it to coincide with 'une vraie vie'. What the narrator discovers is that, in painting the port at Carquethuit, Elstir has done more than provide a sufficient representation of a place so as to make it recognisable; he has gone further and captured in his art the very secret that lies behind the configuration of objects—the town, the boats, the sky—that appear in the painting.

The Hudimesnil episode shows the narrator tormentingly poised on the cusp of recognising what is important to him in this particular configuration of objects—the three trees—that present themselves unexpectedly to his eye. There is also the realisation that there is a secret that he needs to get at and that lies hidden beyond contingent appearance. Proust captures exactly, at this stage in the narrator's development, the itch of curiosity and the sad inadequacy of his having no technique whereby to transform the objects presented to his senses into an imaginatively new correlative to his deepest feelings. The common element in both episodes—the trees at Hudimesnil and Elstir's paintings—is the realisation, through the imagination and therefore in an artistic creation, of the power of transmutation. Metamorphosis is the only way to come to terms with contingent reality, and the resultant spiritual creation is the only means of sharing with others what otherwise would remain forever the secret of the contingent world. The narrator comes very near to understanding that, for a person of the temperament he is gradually discovering himself to be, art is the only justification for life.

The stages of the narrator's experience of the three trees chart not only the steps in his understanding but also, through the great excitement he feels, emphasise the importance of the need to come, if possible, to some concrete creation before the inspirational insight into a secret world disappears. He will at this point fall short, but the lesson does not come to nothing because the Elstir experience, admittedly in paint and not in words, will presently prove the value of what the narrator senses unsurely. Proust establishes at the outset the parallel of overwhelming joy in the Martinville episode and this episode of the three trees. Just as the narrator had experienced coming unexpectedly upon the changing locations of the steeples of Martinville, so here Proust draws attention to the sudden apprehension of the three old trees placed a little way off the switch-back road that the carriage is driving along. The experience is entirely due to chance and the sense of *déjà vu* is all the stronger for being stumbled upon and not sought out: 'mon esprit ayant trébuché entre quelque année lointaine et le moment présent' (II, **92**). The narrator is aware of the objects before him hiding some secret that remains out of his grasp and possibly only attainable if he could be alone and able to work at resolving it, something impossible in the social situation of driving with Mme de Villeparisis in her carriage. The spiritual potential of the situation, however, does not escape him since the pleasure involved, 'que j'avais à créer moi-même', has the power to wipe out the dross of mere existence and put him in touch with 'une vraie vie'. The technique for understanding the phenomenon is to interiorise the trees and set up a series of questions debating their origins, dismissing some things and reconsidering others. This technique of ratiocination applied to the disembodied is something the narrator has already practised in the *madeleine* and the Martinville steeples episodes. The outcome here is most reminiscent of the latter where the narrator attempts by personification to tame the mystery and contain it in words. Here the three trees have a mythical dimension, appearing to him like witches or Norns speaking in riddles, or else like ghosts eager to speak to him but trapped in inarticulacy:

> Je crus plutôt que c'étaient des fantômes du passé, de chers compagnons de mon enfance, des amis disparus qui invoquaient nos communs souvenirs. Comme des ombres ils semblaient me demander de les emmener avec moi, de les rendre à la vie. Dans leur gesticulation naïve et passionnée je reconnaissais le regret impuissant d'un être aimé qui a perdu l'usage de la parole, sent qu'il ne pourra nous dire ce qu'il veut et que nous ne savons pas deviner. (II, **94**)

The impact of his failure of response is felt in the same personified way. The trees wave their arms in desperation and seem to call out: «ce que tu n'apprends pas de nous aujourd'hui tu ne le sauras jamais» (*ibid*). By having to miss the opportunity to pursue his investigation further the narrator feels sad to the point of feeling that a part of himself had died and as if he had turned foolishly away from the divine (*ibid*).

Against this failure to exploit his confrontation with the phenomena of the world of the senses, Proust sets the visit to Elstir's studio and reveals what has to be done to resolve the dilemma of this kind of confrontation. The narrator has already become aware of the trees as changing into things other than trees, such as mythological figures or spirits, and is aware that to speak of them he must perforce use terms other than 'trees'. He even senses that to control them he must give them new names, and that to allow the imagination to function in relation to them is to face the problem of re-naming which necessarily entails allowing an object to become magically something else. Hard reality is but the starting point for a relationship to that reality which is thereafter to be characterised by its fluidity and plasticity.

Though Elstir lives in a rented villa, which is perhaps the ugliest in a suburban part of Balbec noted for its unaesthetic ostentation, the narrator, once he gets inside his studio, feels he can forget the 'laideur citadine' (II, **222**) and make new discoveries as he inspects all the studies for future creations that the painter is currently working on. They transport him from banality to a world where the reality of everday is transfigured. The studio strikes him as a place where reality may be worked upon and transformed from shapelessness into representations that grant their subjects a dignity which extracts their essence while not denying their contingent appearances:

> Et l'atelier d'Elstir m'apparut comme le laboratoire d'une sorte de nouvelle création du monde, où, du chaos que sont toutes choses que nous voyons, il avait tiré, en les peignant sur divers rectangles de toile qui étaient posés dans tous les sens, ici une vague de la mer écrasant avec colère sur le sable son écume lilas, là un jeune homme en coutil blanc accoudé sur le pont d'un bateau. Le veston du jeune homme et la vague éclaboussante avaient pris une dignité nouvelle du fait qu'ils continuaient à être, encore que dépourvus de ce en quoi ils passaient pour consister, la vague ne pouvant plus mouiller, ni le veston habiller personne. (*ibid*)

What lies behind this sense of discovery is something the narrator has already felt earlier in his stay at Balbec and that chimes in with his remarks here, namely, his transformation of the sea with its peaks and troughs into a mountainous landscape (II, **42**) or the way his imagination was made to work to relate the architecture of Carqueville church to the covering of ivy that partly obscured it (II, **89-90**).

As he moves about the studio—described, because of the play of light and shadow, in painterly terms of chiaroscuro: 'je circulais dans ce clair-obscur'—he notices Elstir's seascapes of Balbec and places nearby and their principal stylistic feature which is their power to put across not what the intelligence expects but a re-naming and a re-grouping of their parts, transferring their meaning in the way a metaphor in poetry can bring together the unexpected. He realises that the seascapes are constructed on the principle that 'painting is not the imitation of nature but the *metamorphosis* of nature' (Cocking, p. 75):

> Mais j'y pouvais discerner que le charme de chacune consistait en une
> sorte de métamorphose des choses représentées, analogue à celle qu'en
> poésie on nomme métaphore et que si Dieu le Père avait créé les choses
> en les nommant, c'est en leur ôtant leur nom, ou en leur en donnant un
> autre qu'Elstir les recréait. (II, **223**)

Elstir represents the elements of his scene as they are in essence
without the intervention of the intelligence seeking prosaically to
give them a sensible meaning. The narrator describes his own
sensitivity to this blurring of demarcation that can occur when the
intelligence is in abeyance, such as his confusing of a dark area of sea
with a part of the coastline or his being unsure about a patch of blue
that could belong to sea or sky. He recognises that it is this fertile
vision that Elstir has put into his paintings, that is to say, a vision
where objects speak ambiguously, poetically conveying more than a
single obvious meaning, one of his main metaphors being to compare
land and sea in such a way as to obliterate all demarcation between
them.

The prime example of the technique is the «Port de Carquethuit»
(II, **224-6**), in which the metaphor of presenting the land as sea and
the sea as land in subtle and tireless variations plays precisely on the
mind's desire to maintain the demarcation demanded by
commonsense. The point at which the roofs are 'dépassés [...] par les
mâts' would seem to compensate perhaps for the narrator's
disappointment with Balbec church which, not being on the coast, is
set against 'un fond de maisons aux toits desquelles ne se mêlait
aucun mât' (II, **26**).

In the description of the «Port de Carquethuit» we have the most
elaborate, detailed and lyrical piece of writing in *Jeunes filles*,
providing not only the illusion that such a painting exists (when in it
is nothing more than Proust's words), but also a mimetically
sustained example in the richness of its prose of the metamorphosis
of the contingent world into a re-ordered or re-assembled spiritual
one. While this makes the point about Elstir's vision, the suppleness
and the convolutions of Proust's prose do more than simply refer to
metamorphosis. They allow the reader to experience it even during
reading. Proust realises metamorphosis in words, as Elstir does in
paint, and works in rhythmic convolutions in the way that Elstir
works in contrast and design. Necessarily, Proust has often to resort
to simile, since he is explaining what he sees, but the point is that in
the painting Elstir simply puts contrasting elements side by side with
the directness that is proper to the visual arts. As Elstir blurs the
outlines of sea and shore or makes people seem to be in more than
one place, so Proust's sentences imitate not only the sectioning and
the juxtaposition of contrasting and contradictory elements, but also,

in their meandering, take the reader's eye over the canvas in a way
that brings out the dissolving of one patch of colour into another and
the transformation of the properties of one medium into another, so
that boats look as if they have 'quelque chose de citadin, de construit
sur terre' (II, 224); so that people in different areas seem juxtaposed
to the extent that they give the impression of communicating without
the gap of water between being visible; so that the distant churches of
Criquebec seem to emerge from watery foundations 'dans un
poudroiement de soleil et de vagues' (II, 225); so that in the
foreground of the picture sea and land lose their demarcation, and
men pushing their boats out to sea seem to be as much in the water as
on the wet sand, which in turn takes on the property of water and
mirrors reflections of their vessels; so that the sea is made to follow
the ups and downs of the shoreline and a ship that should sail on the
open sea appears to be floating in the town itself; so that, even more
strangely, women gathering shrimps seem likewise to be down in a
sea-grotto and not on the rocks where they are actually scrabbling;
so that, even more fantastically yet, the sea contrasts with the land by
its swirling energy and sailors on the jetty become so much part of
the wild movement of the sea that they seem to be riding on the back
of a lively animal, and passengers in a boat are thrown about like
people in a rickety cart, with the sailor in charge manning the sail
like a carter with reins as they frolic up and down the slopes of
sunny fields; finally, in the parts of the sea that are calm after the
storm, the reflections become solid and the boats' hulls etherealised:
'... la mer était si calme que les reflets avaient presque plus de
solidité et de réalité que les coques vaporisées par un effet de soleil et
que la perspective faisait s'enjamber les unes les autres' (II, 226).
  The description concludes with a stepping-up of the tempo in a
mass of staccato detail reminiscent of a musical finale, but
impregnated with metaphors that, for instance, transform a ship,
natural to the sea, into a carriage coming out of a ford and shaking
itself dry like an animal. Yet in spite of the transformations taking
place, the refractions, the fragmentations and the wealth of
seemingly contradictory impressions, this multitudinous perception
takes place against a unified element, the sea:

> L'intelligence faisait ensuite un même élément de ce qui était, ici noir dans
> un effet d'orage, plus loin tout d'une couleur avec le ciel et aussi verni
> que lui, et là si blanc de soleil, de brume et d'écume, si compact, si
> terrien, si circonvenu de maisons, qu'on pensait à quelque chaussée de
> pierre ou à un champ de neige, sur lequel on était effrayé de voir un navire
> s'élever en pente raide et à sec comme une voiture qui s'ébroue en sortant
> d'un gué, mais qu'au bout d'un moment, en y voyant sur l'étendue haute
> et inégale du plateau solide des bateaux titubants, on comprenait,
> identique en tous ces aspects divers, être encore la mer. (*ibid*)

So much for the «Port de Carquethuit», but Proust will not leave it there. The *transposition d'art* whereby we have gone from a seemingly original painting into reliving its multiple facets verbally provides momentum for the next phase on art in which the emphasis is more on analysis. While the previous pages were almost entirely lyrically descriptive, now by a procedure typical of Proust we move from the impressionistic to the intellectual side of his writing. He brings the individual quirkiness of art alongside the technologically available creativity of photography in a comparison of the ways of seeing a landscape or seascape. In what way is Elstir's technique and vision justified? In effect, the artist is the pioneer since what he has created has been appropriated by photography, especially where the photographs make us see things in an unexpected way and thus extend in their own fashion a vision of reality that had its origin in art:

> ... image différente de celles que nous avons l'habitude de voir, singulière et pourtant vraie et qui à cause de cela est pour nous doublement saisissante parce qu'elle nous étonne, nous fait sortir de nos habitudes, et tout à la fois nous fait rentrer en nous-même en nous rappelant une impression. [...] Or, l'effort d'Elstir de ne pas exposer les choses telles qu'il savait qu'elles étaient mais selon ces illusions optiques dont notre vision première est faite, l'avait précisément amené à mettre en lumière certaines de ces lois de perspective, plus frappantes alors, car l'art était le premier à les dévoiler. (II, 227)

In a description of another of Elstir's Balbec paintings (II, 227-8), Proust emphasises again the metaphor of land / sea, but also this time their interplay, so as to contrast what the painter may do—by transforming what he sees—and what the photograph—in naturalistic fashion—actually records. The all-embracing eye of the camera can spread out all before us and draw attention especially to contrasts of light. Elstir, however, had already in his transformative vision anticipated this mechanical property of photography and had gone beyond recording impressions of light to exploiting them in re-structuring the reality he observed, so as to use light itself as a metaphor for magical transmutations of all too solid matter. By emphasising the role of light (and consequently of colour), Proust brings out the subtlest and most creative aspect of metamorphosis in Elstir's art, for light, above all else, can transform the material elements of the contingent world and make them interact with each other in an eloquent way. This is the most impressionist feature of Elstir's style and one that the narrator will in fact allude to in describing him in *Sodome et Gomorrhe* as 'le grand impressionniste'. Proust has clearly been drawing on wide-ranging memories of Turner, Monet and Manet among others (Cocking, pp.

146-50). In making these elements 'speak', Elstir is able to reveal not only his stylistic virtuosity in representing them but also, and primarily, his vision of a reality not filled with inert objects. In his vision, even when apparently static, reality is in movement, in a constantly re-arranged state of flux:

> Ces jeux des ombres, que la photographie a banalisés aussi, avaient intéressé Elstir au point qu'il s'était complu autrefois à peindre de véritables mirages, où un château coiffé d'une tour apparaissait comme un château complètement circulaire prolongé d'une tour à son faîte, et en bas d'une tour inverse, soit que la pureté extraordinaire d'un beau temps donnât à l'ombre qui se reflétait dans l'eau la dureté et l'éclat de la pierre, soit que les brumes du matin rendissent la pierre aussi vaporeuse que l'ombre. De même au-delà de la mer, derrière une rangée de bois une autre mer commençait, rosée par le coucher du soleil et qui était le ciel. La lumière inventant comme de nouveaux solides, poussait la coque du bateau qu'elle frappait, en retrait de celle qui était dans l'ombre, et disposait comme les degrés d'un escalier de cristal sur la surface matériellement plane, mais brisée par l'éclairage, de la mer au matin. Un fleuve qui passe sous les ponts d'une ville était pris d'un point de vue tel qu'il apparaissait entièrement disloqué, étalé ici en lac, aminci là en filet, rompu ailleurs par l'interposition d'une colline couronnée de bois où le citadin va le soir respirer la fraîcheur du soir; et le rythme même de cette ville bouleversée n'était assuré que par la verticale inflexible des clochers qui ne montaient pas, mais plutôt, selon le fil à plomb de la pesanteur marquant la cadence comme dans une marche triomphale, semblaient tenir en suspens au-dessous d'eux toute la masse plus confuse des maisons étagées dans la brume, le long du fleuve écrasé et décousu. (II, 228)

This is Elstir's creative vision which the narrator learns to decipher and to admire and in which there is not only the play of light dissolving reality but also a rearrangement of planes that suggests a cubist restructuring of the landscape (cf. Uenishi, p. 100). But what is there in practical terms that can help him in his progress towards his *vocation invisible*? The narrator cannot vie with Elstir. He cannot paint, but he can see. What Elstir spiritually instructs him in is precisely what an artist can best do: teach him to see, see anew, and this is what he does in talking to him about looking at Balbec church. The way the narrator had previously seen it won't do; it must be transformed into a lesson of openness to metamorphosis, to seeing the medium of stone as transcending the modelling of the individual figures. As he had done with Charlus, Proust knows the moment to let a character talk, so here Elstir explains at length (II, 229-31) what the narrator had missed when looking at the porch of Balbec church. Elstir eloquently tumbles out all the interconnecting graphic detail of the sculptures that adorn the porch, mingling his demotic 'chouette' with the clearly and accurately retailed descriptions of every attitude and gesture of the Virgin and those

who attend her—'Car c'est tous les cercles du ciel, tout un
gigantesque poème théologique et symbolique que vous avez là' (II,
230). Even the Oriental element the narrator had expected to find,
and was disappointed with being unable to detect, was there all along.
Elstir can confirm that, to anyone who looks closely, even that
element is there: 'un chapiteau reproduit si exactement un sujet
persan que la persistance des traditions orientales ne suffit pas à
l'expliquer' (II, **231**). The work, in fact, is a loving exercise in
transformation where everything, for all the diversity, has its place
and where all the separate elements can be read in an integrated way.
This is no exercise in stone-carving but a spiritual re-creation
through the medium of sculpture of something the sculptor worked
at and by artistic effort turned from contingent material into
spiritual experience: 'la plus belle Bible historiée que le peuple ait
jamais pu lire' (II, **229**). The mediaeval artist is compared at this
point with Odilon Redon, who wrote that, over and above objective
reality which provides a starting point, essentially 'l'art véritable est
dans la réalité *sentie*' (cited II, **380**). Indeed, in matters involving the
imaginative understanding of the world and one's impressions of it
Elstir brooks no half-measures. He provides a further brief lesson.
He not only teaches the narrator to see but recommends also the full
indulgence of fantasy: 'tout le rêve'. A little imagination is a
dangerous thing, allowing only a superficial understanding of one's
dreams for which the only solution is a thoroughgoing acceptance of
this faculty: 'Il importe qu'on connaisse entièrement ses rêves pour
n'en plus souffrir' (II, **232**).

While he is still in Elstir's studio, the narrator becomes aware that
the spiritual dimension of Elstir's work imbues not only the sublime,
as in the big lyrical canvases or the paean of praise to the anonymous
mediaeval sculptor, but also the human, everyday side of life. His
impulse towards the indulgence of the imagination, and its
consequent expression in his technique of altering appearances so as
to provoke equivocal responses, is reflected even in the banal and the
domestic. The narrator is surprised and intrigued by an old water-
colour of Elstir's depicting a young woman in a pose and costume
suggesting a young man, an ambiguous figure 'en demi-travesti' (II,
238). It is precisely the ambiguity that has attracted Elstir as 'un
élément esthétique qui valait d'être mis en relief' (II, **239**). The
transformation of the expected by emphasising the unexpected
clearly dates from early on in his career. He makes a point here of
capturing the in-between characteristics; is the figure 'une fille un
peu garçonnière' or 'un jeune efféminé vicieux et songeur' (*ibid*)?
The work is called *Miss Sacripant* and turns out to be Odette as a
character from an operetta (II, **251**). On a more homely level, the

narrator encounters a similar instance of transformation and
transfiguration through art in the case of Mme Elstir. When she
turns up at the studio she appears to the narrator to be
unprepossessing, heavy, inelegant and somewhat coarse in looks.
Later, however, when he appreciates Elstir's mythological style he
sees her as attractive because transformed in art in her husband's
paintings of her. What the narrator had perceived as her banality is
transmuted and a spiritual quality replaces the contingent: 'son corps
perdit de sa lourdeur, car je le remplis d'une idée, l'idée qu'elle était
une créature immatérielle, un portrait d'Elstir' (II, **241**).

Finally in *Jeunes filles* there is the moment when the narrator
learns how Elstir's art can bring him the joy of relating to objects
whose very inertness has, by the trick of style in presenting them,
been turned into emotion. Just as Mme Elstir is lifted to a non-
material plane merely by being part of Elstir's vision, so everyday
objects of no importance become objects of beauty in themselves.
Reflecting on Elstir's water-colours, the narrator begins to
appreciate the beauty inherent in his still-life studies. What would
otherwise have been disregarded as too banal for any attention takes
on a beauty precisely because transfigured by Elstir's art. In these
still-lifes, Elstir is able to allude to the secrets that lie within the
objects observed and, while being lucidly exact and representational,
to play on the colour changes brought about by light. The narrator
speaks of *déplacement, transmutation* and *altération,* and is led to
extend his understanding of the objects on the table by resorting to
metaphors that interpret the remains of the meal as ritual, the table
itself as altar, the droplets in the oysters as *gouttes d'eau lustrale* and
their shells as tiny stone fonts. Elstir brings off a double: his realistic
still-life captures not only the sheer actuality of what he depicts but
also paradoxically the living secret existence of a *nature morte*:

> Depuis que j'en avais vu dans les aquarelles d'Elstir, je cherchais à
> retrouver dans la réalité, j'aimais comme quelque chose de poétique, le
> geste interrompu des couteaux encore de travers, la rondeur bombée d'une
> serviette défaite où le soleil intercale un morceau de velours jaune, le verre
> à demi vidé qui montre mieux ainsi le noble évasement de ses formes et au
> fond de son vitrage translucide et pareil à une condensation du jour, un
> reste de vin sombre mais scintillant de lumières, le déplacement des
> volumes, la transmutation des liquides par l'éclairage, l'altération des
> prunes qui passent du vert au bleu et du bleu à l'or dans le compotier déjà
> à demi dépouillé, la promenade des chaises vieillottes qui deux fois par
> jour viennent s'installer autour de la nappe, dressée sur la table ainsi que
> sur un autel où sont célébrées les fêtes de la gourmandise et sur laquelle au
> fond des huîtres quelques gouttes d'eau lustrale restent comme dans de
> petits bénitiers de pierre; j'essayais de trouver la beauté là où je ne m'étais
> jamais figuré qu'elle fût, dans les choses les plus usuelles, dans la vie
> profonde des «natures mortes». (II, **261-2**)

Where is all this tending? How eventually will it bear fruit for the narrator? Elstir has shown him how to set about confronting reality by drawing attention to the the the artist's duty to go beyond realistic appearances and rearrange the observed world so as to bring out a greater truth about it. This truth lies not in objectivity, but in a deep personal meditation that transforms, even distorts, what is apparent, thereby making the artist's subjective traffic with appearances available as a design, a creation in its own right. The reason why it is Elstir's painting that, of all artistic discoveries, speaks to the narrator is that temperamentally he is inclined, without as yet being fully aware of it, to share Elstir's aesthetic ideal, that is to say, the transferring of what would otherwise be unknown and unshared into the general consciousness. Appearances as such cannot do this, but work done to those appearances by subjecting them to the analytical eye of the artist can transform the banal into the meaningful by an act of intuitive insight capable of linking the unlikely in a logic of its own. The phenomenon of transference by means of analogies can make a parallel emerge where none was expected and, by the surprise and aptness of the connection, provide a progression beyond appearances that can lead to a sense of elation enough to lift us from flat contingency or even mortality.

The narrator does not re-experience that feeling, evoked in *Combray* at the time of the *madeleine* incident, of ceasing to feel 'médiocre, contingent, mortel' (*Swann,* **142**) until he fully appreciates the message in *Le Temps retrouvé* that will lead him to literary creation. However, in the visit to the restaurant at Rivebelle just before the narrator meets Elstir, Proust does provide a small-scale example of an experience pregnant with the transformative inventiveness of imagination acting on material of the most banal kind. This transformation scene is a taster for the grander notion of metamorphosis the narrator is about to discover on examining Elstir's canvases. At Rivebelle, carried away by the gipsy music in the restaurant, the narrator, who is in a pleasant relaxed state—and certainly not drunk!—begins to see the tables turning in the sheer hustle and bustle of the restaurant and transformed into revolving planets such as might figure in old allegorical pictures from the Middle Ages. Already he makes comparisons between his vision of the world and what a painter might see and create. Even before the revelation of Elstir's studio, Proust draws parallels between writing and painting, something particularly relevant at this point since, just before going to the restaurant, the narrator has been thinking about realising himself as a writer like Bergotte and is conscious of 'l'œuvre que je portais peut-être en moi' (II, **194**). For writer or painter the answer is not in the notation of what presents itself to the eye but in its transformation. This is what the narrator—more instinctively than intellectually—does when he describes the restaurant as full of 'tables astrales' and the two horrible women at the till as grotesque sorceresses: 'deux magiciennes occupées à prévoir par des calculs astrologiques les bouleversements qui pouvaient parfois se produire dans cette voûte céleste conçue selon la science du Moyen Age' (II, **196**). Though carried away by his own vision, he is aware that it is not shared with the other diners; only its recording in a work of art could allow that sharing—which the reader has paradoxically, as it happens, just experienced—because only then by a process of analysis and reassembly can the essence of the scene be transferred from the artist to the receiver by the intermediary of analogical associations:

> Et je plaignais un peu tous les dîneurs parce que je sentais que pour eux les tables rondes n'étaient pas des planètes et qu'ils n'avaient pas pratiqué dans les choses *un sectionnement qui nous débarrasse de leur apparence coutumière* et nous permet d'apercevoir des *analogies*. (II, **196-7**; my emphasis)

In this scene, which precedes the narrator's discovery of the power of metaphor in Elstir's seascapes, we are put through the whole process of being presented with an aesthetically unpromising situation precisely by a metaphor. Proust resorts to a methaphor of movement in a non-terrestrial space that must be at the furthest possible remove from people enjoying themselves with food and drink. If presently it will dawn on the narrator that Elstir has seen land in terms of water and water in terms of land, certainly here, without fully tumbling to what he has done, the narrator has seen a busy dining-room, its individual tables and swirling waiters, in terms of a celestial harmony of moving bodies. At this point the narrator stands back and makes the intellectual observation quoted above, to the effect that the diners, who do not see the scene as he does, cannot share in the aesthetic dimension which the narrator's imagination has accorded events by magically transforming them. Having made clear the potential artist's view, Proust immediately resumes the scene, having benefited from the metaphor, in a description that rhythmically continues to imitate the swirling movements of the waiters mechanically immersed in the banal round of their duties.

A little later Proust provides yet another metaphor in a transformation scene that brings him near to what he is shortly to learn is a particular feature of Elstir's technique: the God-like renaming of parts. In another section of the restaurant at Rivebelle, in 'une longue galerie vitrée', the narrator transforms the 'goûteuses', as they appear in the intermittent light streaming

through the long corridor and its occasional open panels, into a
flutter of shimmering fragments. From being given the facts about
the section of the restaurant set aside for *goûters* we arrive
unexpectedly at a miniature painting in which the prosaic solidity of
reality is broken up into refracting pieces by the emphasis on the
element most dear to any painter and especially to Elstir, the play of
light. What begins as a glazed corridor ends in fragmented details
where the image of the *goûteuses* is almost dissolved away and their
movements arrested as if in a still-life. The reader arrives at the
éclatants poissons by surprise, no direct simile is used, but a
metaphor replaces the banal image of the *goûteuses* with one
combining light and fluidity. The narrator has taken everyday
elements and, prefiguring Elstir, renamed them (II, **199**).

Though it will take the narrator some good time yet before
aesthetic lessons converge with the right moment for him to see in
art the justification for his existence in *Le Temps retrouvé*, the
principles have been set already—the little essay on the Martinville
steeples, the sense of a need to search beyond the appearances of the
three trees, the revelation of metamorphosis in Elstir and even of
metaphor itself in Bergotte. Describing Bergotte's prose style and his
other literary strategies, the narrator has already distilled the most
important ingredient for any creator: intellectual distinction and
conventional taste are secondary to the transformative power of the
imagination, something he goes on to illustrate metaphorically:

> Mais le génie, même le grand talent, vient moins d'éléments intellectuels
> et d'affinement social supérieurs à ceux d'autrui, que de la faculté de les
> transformer, de les transposer. Pour faire chauffer un liquide avec une
> lampe électrique, il ne s'agit pas d'avoir la plus forte lampe possible,
> mais une dont le courant puisse cesser d'éclairer, être dérivé et donner,
> au lieu de lumière, de la chaleur. (I, **228**)

The importance, above all, of the relationship of what is in the
eye of the beholder to what in fact is beheld in the contingent world,
has emerged in 'le pouvoir réfléchissant' (I, **229**) and is reinforced
in the narrator's resuming of his acquaintance with Elstir's paintings
in the gallery of the duc de Guermantes. In the painting referred to
as 'fête au bord de l'eau' the narrator discovers how Elstir succeeds
in uniting in its patterning of light both the picturesque (meaning
what is conventionally worthy of bring represented in art) and the
banal and unpromising, i.e. both the scene of the boats, on the one
hand, and the overdressed lady, on the other. The narrator comes to
realise that beauty lies not in instrinsic items but in the overall
transformation brought about by the painter's imagination:

... cette femme est belle aussi, sa robe reçoit la même lumière que la
voile du bateau, il n'y a pas de choses plus ou moins précieuses, la robe
commune et la voile en elle-même jolie sont deux miroirs du même
reflet. Tout le prix est dans les regards du peintre. (Pléiade II, 421)

Elstir, whether at Balbec or elsewhere, constantly provides the
potential writer with pointers for the future. By being true to his
imagination he has always succeeded in capturing the immediacy of
the scene and provided the evidence that creation, of any kind, is
making a shape where previously there was, if not outright chaos,
then at least nondescript disorder. He gives life to Coleridge's
definition in the "Dejection Ode":

> ... what Nature gave me at my Birth,
> My shaping Spirit of Imagination.

Subjectivity is all. The technique of analogies used to transmit that
subjectivity is not a mere parallelism—what was sea is now land, for
example—but a new relationship to the totality of the scene so that
what the painting creates is a picture that is impossible in life. It is
the energy released by bringing the contradictories together that is
important, thereby releasing in turn the essence inherent in the
reality of the scene, but hidden until the artist's associations and
optical distortions cause us to be caught up in rethinking what we are
looking at. We are simultaneously in the world of the contingent
shapes of a given scene and sharing the deeper possibilities of those
shapes through the subjective intuiting of the artist. The sense of
transformation is such that there is the same pleasure in the resulting
duality as the narrator describes in relation to involuntary memories,
which he characterises as being 'réels sans être actuels, idéaux sans
être abstraits' (*Le Temps retrouvé*, **263**). Of all the insights the
narrator experiences, it is the painterly view, that leads him to the
crucial discussion of metaphor and style in *Le Temps retrouvé*.

The narrator, in his older and wiser voice, gives ample evidence
throughout *La Recherche* of being a painterly writer, and in parts of
Jeunes filles of being an impressionist one. Just before the narrator
differentiates Albertine from the group of girls, he depicts the whole
scene in a way that captures the very essence of imprecision as well
as the immediacy of impression. Describing the regulation parade of
the elegant *estivants* of Balbec proceeding along the seawall, he
captures the energy that ripples through the assembly of people as
they pose and turn, admire and criticise. Exploiting to the full his
proclivity to the meandering sentence, including therein an example
of the expressive parenthesis for which his style is famous, Proust
mimics their movement and captures at the same time their self-

importance and their self-regarding vanity with all the freshness of a
Boudin:

> Tous ces gens qui longeaient la digue en tanguant aussi fort que si elle
> avait été le pont d'un bateau (car ils ne savaient pas lever une jambe sans
> du même coup remuer le bras, tourner les yeux, remettre d'aplomb leurs
> épaules, compenser par un mouvement balancé du côté opposé le
> mouvement qu'ils venaient de faire de l'autre côté, et congestionner leur
> face) et qui, faisant semblant de ne pas voir, pour faire croire qu'ils ne
> se souciaient pas d'elles, mais regardant à la dérobée, pour ne pas
> risquer de les heurter, les personnes qui marchaient à leurs côtés ou
> venaient en sens inverse, butaient au contraire contre elles,
> s'accrochaient à elles, parce qu'ils avaient été réciproquement de leur
> part l'objet de la même attention secrète, cachée sous le même dédain
> apparent; l'amour—par conséquent la crainte—de la foule étant un des
> plus puissants mobiles chez tous les hommes, soit qu'ils cherchent à
> plaire aux autres ou à les étonner, soit à leur montrer qu'ils les
> méprisent. (II, **172**)

It is among these figures that he catches sight of the group of
girls, who are for the moment undifferentiated and moving freely
'sans hésitation ni raideur', but in a co-ordinated collective way that
marks them off from the crowd. The narrator's perception of detail
is restricted to atomised features—this one's dark skin, that one's
laughing eyes, another's shining rosy cheeks. Though Proust makes a
reference to music as evoking the blending of these details, it is
interesting to see how the main metaphor is painting. Sometimes he
blurs the two and refers to 'toutes les gammes de couleurs', but in
the main he is thinking of the effects of details in a painting, for
example, 'un roi Mage de type arabe' in a Renaissance canvas. The
girls are a blend of colours and movement, precisely such as would
be found in an impressionist work, with colours the principal
feature—*ovale blanc, yeux noirs, yeux verts*. The confusion of
details, especially in their colour, is juxtaposed as if in a pointillist
style, which is rounded off in phrases that imitate the arabesques of
movement and point to the narrator's escape from the banality of the
morning constitutional into seeing the girls as a transmutation of
their collective beauty:

> Et cette absence, dans ma vision, des démarcations que j'établirais
> bientôt entre elles, propageait à travers leur groupe un flottement
> harmonieux, la translation continue d'une beauté fluide, collective et
> mobile. (II, **173-4**)

It is evident that there is a deep level at which what the narrator
discovers through Elstir's paintings is already within his own
sensibility and even in his instinctual vision of the world around him.
He is already inclined to see the world in the painterly way of Elstir

and, as the above extracts show, able to accommodate individual details in a cohesive whole. As we read the description of the people walking on the sea wall with the group of girls moving through them, it is as if our eyes are being tracked like a cine camera over a canvas, giving now the broad view, now zooming in to highlight a detail. The narrator comes close to the ideal he is eventually supposed to find only in *Le Temps retrouvé*. Since, however, the economy of the work demands the demonstration of an evolution, all we get at first are suggestions—very pregnant ones, as it happens. In building up to his grand revelation Proust must have as the nodal point in the whole phenomenon of metamorphosis a character, not at this point a writer, who can put before us, in one plane as in a painting, to be seen at a glance, all that the potential writer wishes to do to realise his invisible vocation. For his communication in words the writer needs, like the musician, space and time, whereas the painter can show all at once. It is, therefore, most apt to have as principal intermediary in the problems of transformation a painter whose canvases graphically show the parallel problems of language in revealing the need to devise a discourse that can work on many levels simultaneously. It is the sheer painterliness of Vermeer that the dying Bergotte is led ultimately to understand when he makes the effort to go to the exhibition to see the patch of yellow wall in Vermeer's *View of Delft*. In giving precedence to the painter's technique and vision, Bergotte confirms for the narrator that the true guide for him as a writer is this painterly view of style made evident for him in the example of Elstir (cf. Mavrakis, p. 178):

> «C'est ainsi que j'aurais dû écrire, disait-il. Mes derniers livres sont trop secs, il aurait fallu passer plusieurs couches de couleur, rendre ma phrase en elle-même précieuse, comme ce petit pan de mur jaune». (*La Prisonnière*, **285**)

When the narrator in *Le Temps retrouvé* moves to his final successful revelation regarding his mode of operation, it will be by devices that face metamorphosis head-on, in particular metaphor. Surface description can proceed indefinitely but can never take us beyond that restricted level of information, since the very directness of the process fails to breed comparison, and variability, fails to lift us out of the sensation of the contingent and fails above all to understand the interfolding of contradictions in our sensations and memories that only art can resolve:

> On peut faire se succéder indéfiniment dans une description les objets qui figuraient dans le lieu décrit; la vérité ne commencera qu'au moment où l'écrivain prendra deux objets différents, posera leur rapport, analogue dans le monde de l'art à celui qu'est le rapport unique de la loi

> causale dans le monde de la science, et les enfermera dans les anneaux nécessaires d'un beau style. Même ainsi que la vie quand en rapprochant une qualité commune à deux sensations, il dégagera leur essence commune en les réunissant l'une et l'autre pour les soustraire aux contingences du temps, dans une métaphore. La nature ne m'avait-elle pas mis elle-même à ce point de vue sur la voie de l'art, n'était-elle pas commencement d'art elle-même, elle qui ne m'avait permis de connaître souvent la beauté d'une chose que dans une autre [...] ? La vérité ne commencera qu'au moment où l'écrivain prendra deux objets différents, posera leur rapport, et les enchaînera par le lien indestructible d'une alliance de mots. (*Le Temps retrouvé*, **282-3**)

Recording reality without transforming it—'la littérature de notations'—is inadequate. For the writer, true reality is locked in past impressions which must be brought forth and transfigured. The painter can operate the technique of restructuring simply by manipulating the view before him; the writer, however, has to use as *his* raw material what has gone from view but, thanks to Memory, foremost of the Muses, is nevertheless not lost. Proust clinches the importance of what Elstir has stood for in the mind of the narrator when he defines the writer's task as being the equivalent of the painter's. Only literature can penetrate to the narrator's 'vraie vie' and the route is via understanding that style is not mere dilettante decoration:

> La vraie vie, la vie enfin découverte et éclaircie, la seule vie par conséquent réellement vécue, c'est la littérature. Cette vie qui en un sens, habite à chaque instant chez tous les hommes aussi bien que chez l'artiste. Mais ils ne la voient pas, parce qu'ils ne cherchent pas à l'éclaircir. Et ainsi leur passé est encombré d'innombrables clichés qui restent inutiles parce que l'intelligence ne les a pas «développés». Notre vie; et aussi la vie des autres car le style pour l'écrivain aussi bien que la couleur pour le peintre est une question non de technique mais de vision. (*Le Temps retrouvé*, **289**)

In many ways Proust could be said to subscribe to a remark Maeterlinck makes in his essay on Novalis in *Le Trésor des humbles:*

> Une vérité cachée est ce qui nous fait vivre.

Proust knew Maeterlinck's essays and could well have read these words. Is this not the dynamic behind the concern with style and vision that the narrator discovers through Elstir? Is this not what gives his own quest for lost time its impetus?

Conclusion

A l'ombre des jeunes filles en fleurs, especially if we allow *Noms de pays: le nom* to serve as a third panel to *Autour de Mme Swann* and *Noms de pays: le pays,* can be appreciated as a triptych representing an adolescent from a protected and privileged world who is just at the point of emerging into the arena of first maturity. He is depicted as poised between two female figures, Gilberte and Albertine, and becoming painfully independent as he sheds his older female protectors, Françoise and his mother. There is a mythic, initiatory feel to *Jeunes filles,* in which the young man goes out into a world where he will meet tribulations of various kinds, but will also find that guides are placed in his path. For all his doubts, there is nevertheless a sense of progression towards an ultimate successful self-realisation, in the best tradition of the man who seeks his fortune by dint of undertaking a great search, only to find that all along it lay within him.

In the broad design of *La Recherche,* the over-protected child of *Combray* begins to emerge into the interesting and ambiguous territory of growing away from the family. This comes about in terms of sexuality and also in terms of understanding how sensibility must be related to artistic realisation. The twin problems of personal relationships and an ever deeper investigation into the inmost self's perception of the world are consistently played off one against the other. The earliest and tenderest exposure to the world, as shown in *Combray,* has been hardened as sophistication begins to temper naïveté. At first the narrator's sensibility is primarily and naturally self-centred and self-indulgent. His involvement with Gilberte shows the naïve self finding it hard to come to terms with another individual. With Albertine, there is a deeper sexual commitment that would seem to hold promise, though even in *Noms de pays: le pays* there are suggestions that the equivalence of one individual to another will not be simple. Above all, the narrator, even though drawn to seeking a progression from self-centredness to shared experience, inherently feels that the introspective demands of realising his own sensibility to the full will take precedence. Already with Saint-Loup he feels that friendship must take second place to realising his potential for artistic achievement. As the reader attempts to look ahead to further emotional developments, it is evident that, as far as the narrator is concerned, the lesson of Elstir must first be appreciated; once learned, then farewell commitment to others, for to be married is to be married to his art.

Biographical Table

1871	Proust born at Auteuil, Paris, 10 July.
1871	Childhood holidays, continuing till 1886, at Illiers.
1881	First attack of asthma, which thereafter rules his life.
1882-1889	Attends Lycée Condorcet.
1889	Military service as volunteer at Orléans. September holiday in Cabourg, Normandy.
1890-1891	Matriculates in Law Faculty and at École des Sciences Politiques.
1892-1893	Contributes to *Le Banquet,* founded by himself and friends, and also to *La Revue blanche*
1893	Licence en Droit. Prepares for an arts degree with view to librarianship.
1894	Liaison with Reynaldo Hahn (till 1896).
1895	Licence ès Lettres (Philosophie). Frequents fashionable salons. Given sinecure post as librarian at Bibliothèque Mazarine. Holiday with Hahn in Normandy (Dieppe) and Brittany (Beg-Meil). Begins *Jean Santeuil,* using in part his holiday memories.
1896	Publishes first book: *Les Plaisirs et les Jours*; luxury edition at his own expense, collecting together most of his poems, sketches and stories published to date.
1897	Duel (exchange of shots) with Jean Lorrain who had attacked him over his relationship with Lucien Daudet.
1898	Zola's *J'accuse...!* reopens the Dreyfus Case (begun in 1894). Proust signs the *L'Aurore* petition for a retrial.
1899	Begins study of Ruskin and translates *The Bible of Amiens.*
1900	Memorial articles on death of Ruskin. Visits Venice in April (with his mother) and again in October. Continues work on Ruskin.

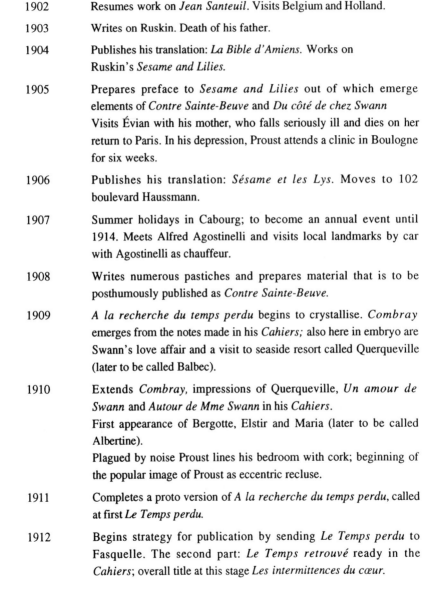

1901   Further study of Ruskin with visits to Amiens and Abbeville. Recurrence of asthma.

1902   Resumes work on *Jean Santeuil*. Visits Belgium and Holland.

1903   Writes on Ruskin. Death of his father.

1904   Publishes his translation: *La Bible d'Amiens*. Works on Ruskin's *Sesame and Lilies*.

1905   Prepares preface to *Sesame and Lilies* out of which emerge elements of *Contre Sainte-Beuve* and *Du côté de chez Swann*
Visits Évian with his mother, who falls seriously ill and dies on her return to Paris. In his depression, Proust attends a clinic in Boulogne for six weeks.

1906   Publishes his translation: *Sésame et les Lys*. Moves to 102 boulevard Haussmann.

1907   Summer holidays in Cabourg; to become an annual event until 1914. Meets Alfred Agostinelli and visits local landmarks by car with Agostinelli as chauffeur.

1908   Writes numerous pastiches and prepares material that is to be posthumously published as *Contre Sainte-Beuve*.

1909   *A la recherche du temps perdu* begins to crystallise. *Combray* emerges from the notes made in his *Cahiers;* also here in embryo are Swann's love affair and a visit to seaside resort called Querqueville (later to be called Balbec).

1910   Extends *Combray,* impressions of Querqueville, *Un amour de Swann* and *Autour de Mme Swann* in his *Cahiers*.
First appearance of Bergotte, Elstir and Maria (later to be called Albertine).
Plagued by noise Proust lines his bedroom with cork; beginning of the popular image of Proust as eccentric recluse.

1911   Completes a proto version of *A la recherche du temps perdu*, called at first *Le Temps perdu*.

1912   Begins strategy for publication by sending *Le Temps perdu* to Fasquelle. The second part: *Le Temps retrouvé* ready in the *Cahiers*; overall title at this stage *Les intermittences du cœur*.

1912   *Le Temps perdu*, rejected by Fasquelle, is submitted to Gallimard but
            also rejected for the NRF imprint by Gide.
            Extracts from *Le Temps perdu* published in *Le Figaro* .
            Puts finishing touches to *Le Côté de Guermantes* in his *Cahiers*.

1913   Submitted to Ollendorf, the novel is rejected a third time.
            Proposes his work to Grasset for publication at author's expense.
            Céleste Albaret taken on as housekeeper and is to remain devotedly
            to the end. Employs Agostinelli as secretary.
            By mid-May agrees on new overall title for novel: *A la recherche
            du temps perdu*. On 14 November publication of *Du côté de chez
            Swann*. Gives important pre-publication interview to Élie-Joseph
            Bois in *Le Temps* on 13 November, and a second promotional
            interview to André Arnyvelde in *Le Miroir* on 21 December.
            Agostinelli disappears and goes to Antibes to train as a pilot,
            adopting as cover the name Marcel Swann; is pursued by Proust
            through an intermediary in the hope that he might return.
            Proust completes *Le Côte de Guermantes* and a second episode set
            at the seaside; first appearance of Albertine.

1914   Agostinelli killed in air crash the very day Proust writes to say he
            has bought him a plane for 27,000 francs. Prepares a first version of
            La Prisonnière and *La Fugitive*.
            Rejected for war service.

1915   *Sodome et Gomorrhe*, *La Prisonnière* and *La Fugitive* developed
            in seven *Cahiers*.
            Letter in November to Mme Scheikévitch sketches out Albertine
            story. Albertine brought into the first stay at Balbec, then into
            Sodome et Gomorrhe for second stay at Balbec, and finally her
            flight described.

1916   Gide repents of his folly in rejecting *Du côté de chez Swann*.
            Whole novel to be published henceforth by Gallimard and the NRF.
            Proust becomes less reclusive, resumes the social round, but also
            frequents less respectable milieux, including Le Cuziat's *maison de
            bains*.

1917   Further socialising. Gallimard's new edition of *Du côté de chez
            Swann* in readiness but not distributed because of the war.

1917	*A l'ombre des jeunes filles en fleurs* in proof stage.
1918	Corrects proofs of *A l'ombre des jeunes filles en fleurs* and completes drafting *A la recherche du temps perdu.* Despite health problems, socialises; associates with Ritz waiter Henri Rochat.
1918	*A l'ombre des jeunes fillles en fleurs* ready for publication.
1919	Rochat taken on as secretary and provides some elements of Albertine. *A l'ombre des jeunes filles en fleurs* published in June together with *Du côté de chez Swann* and *Pastiches et Mélanges.*
1919	In October, obliged to move to a fifth floor apartment at 44 rue Hamelin, looked after by the faithful Céleste. In December, receives Prix Goncourt by a narrow majority for *A l'ombre des jeunes filles en fleurs.*
1920	*Le Côté de Guermantes I.*
1921	*Le Côté de Guermantes II* and *Sodome et Gomorrhe I.* Health deteriorates.
1922	*Sodome et Gomorrhe II.* Proust dies on 18 November from pneumonia and neglect, correcting his novel to the end.
1923	*La Prisonnière* brought out by Jacques Rivière and Proust's brother Robert.
1924	*Les Plaisirs et les Jours* reissued.
1925	*Albertine disparue;* later retitled *La Fugitive .*
1927	*Le Temps retrouvé .*
1928	*Chroniques* (articles brought together by Robert Proust).
1952	*Jean Santeuil.*
1954	*Contre Sainte-Beuve,* with *Nouveaux Mélanges .*

Select Bibliography

Editions

A la recherche du temps perdu, ed. by J.-Y. Tadié *et al.,* 4 vols. Paris: Gallimard, Bibliothèque de la Pléiade, 1987-1989.

A la recherche du temps perdu, ed. by Pierre Clarac & André Ferré, 3 vols. Paris: Gallimard, Bibliothèque de la Pléiade, 1954.

A l'ombre des jeunes filles en fleurs, ed. with introduction and notes by Danièle Gasiglia-Laster, 2 vols. Paris: Garnier-Flammarion, 1987.

A l'ombre des jeunes filles en fleurs, ed. with introduction and notes by Pierre-Louis Rey, 1 vol. Paris: Gallimard, 1988.

Contre Sainte-Beuve, with *Pastiches et mélanges* and *Essais et articles,* ed. Pierre Clarac & Yves Sandre. Paris: Gallimard, Bibliothèque de la Pléiade, 1971.

Correspondance, ed. Philip Kolb, 21 vols. Paris: Plon, 1970-1993.

Jean Santeuil, and *Les Plaisirs et les Jours,* ed. by Pierre Clarac & Yves Sandre. Paris: Gallimard, Bibliothèque de la Pléiade, 1971.

Textes retrouvés, ed. by Philip Kolb & L.B. Price. Urbana: University of Illinois Press, 1968.

Books

Biographical Studies

Albaret, C.	*Monsieur Proust.* Paris: Laffont, 1973.
Hayman, R.	*Marcel Proust.* London: Heinemann, 1990.
Mauriac, C.	*Proust par lui-même.* Paris: Seuil, 1953.

| Maurois, A. | *A la recherche de Marcel Proust.* Paris: Hachette, 1949. |
| Painter, G.D. | *Marcel Proust.* London: Chatto & Windus, 2 vols., 1959, 1965. |

Critical Studies

Bardèche, M.	*Marcel Proust romancier.* Paris :Les Sept Couleurs, 2 vols., 1971.
Bersani, L.	*Proust: The Fictions of Life and Art.* Oxford University Press, 1965.
Chernowitz, M.-E.	*Proust and Painting.* New York: International M.C. Univ. Press, 1945.
Cocking, J.M.	*Proust.* Cambridge University Press, 1982.
Deleuze, G.	*Proust et les signes.* Paris: P.U.F., 1976.
Graham, W.	*The Imagery of Proust.* Oxford: Blackwell, 1966.
Green, F.C.	*The Mind of Proust.* Cambridge University Press, 1949.
Henry, A. (1)	*Proust: théories pour une esthétique.* Paris: Klincksieck, 1981.
Henry, A. (2)	*Proust: une vie, une oeuvre, une époque.* Paris: Balland, 1986.
Hughes, E.J.	*Proust: a study in the quality of awareness.* Cambridge Univ. Press, 1983.
Monnin-Hornung. J.	*Proust et la peinture.* Genève: Droz, 1951.
Minogue, V.	*Proust: 'Du côté de chez Swann'.* London: Arnold, 1973.
Poulet, G. (1)	*Études sur le temps humain.* Paris: Plon, 1949.

Poulet, G. (2)   *L'Espace proustien*. Paris: Gallimard, 1963.

Rogers, B.G.   *Proust's Narrative Technique*. Geneva: Droz, 1956.

Stern, S.   *Swann's Way*. Cambridge University Press, 1989.

Tadié, J.-Y.   *Proust et le roman*. Paris: Gallimard, 1971.

Uenishi, T.   *Le Style de Proust et la peinture*. Paris: SEDES, 1988.

Articles

Black, C.J.   'Albertine as an allegorical figure of time', *Romanic Review*, 54 (1963), 171-86.

Genette, G.   'Proust palimpseste', *Tel Quel*,.12 (1963), 60-72.

Mavrakis, A.   'Les Leçons de la peinture: Proust et l'*ut pictura poesis*', *Poétique*, 94 (1993), 171-84.

Whiteley, J. D.   'Marcel and Gilberte—an unpublished episode from the Proust manuscripts', *Essays in French Literature*, 20 (1983), 20-29.

Willis, S.   '«Gilbertine» apparue', *Romanic Review*, 73 (1982), 331-45.